W9-DII-141

Essays on Rhetorical Criticism

Consulting Editor: DON GEIGER

University of California, Berkeley

NEW YORK

Essays ON
Rhetorical Criticism

THOMAS R. NILSEN, Editor

University of Washington

RANDOM HOUSE

First Printing

© Copyright, 1968, by Random House, Inc.
© Copyright, 1957, by Western Speech Association

All rights reserved under International and Pan-American
Copyright Conventions. Published in New York by Random
House, Inc. and simultaneously in Toronto, Canada, by
Random House of Canada Limited.

Library of Congress Catalog Card Number: 68–13156

Manufactured in the United States of America

TO *Ernest J. Wrage*

Preface

In the spring of 1957 an entire issue of *Western Speech* was devoted to a group of essays under the title "Criticism and Public Address," planned by guest editor Ernest J. Wrage, Professor of Speech at Northwestern University. In his brief introduction to the essays Dr. Wrage expressed his appreciation for having been invited to prepare the issue and commented:

> No strings were attached to the invitation to plan this issue. I was a free agent and therefore might have devoted these pages to some problem in scholarship other than criticism. But if I judge correctly, a preponderance of our collective scholarship falls under the general heading of historical-critical studies. Also I am of the opinion that we still need to learn much, much more about the theory, methods, and values of criticism if we are to produce increasingly significant studies. I believe that the papers in this journal will add to our vision and knowledge, that they live up to the title by offering perspectives that enrich the literature of criticism.

The essays have worn well, and after a decade it is appropriate to bring them out in a more permanent and readily available form. Republication in a volume also affords the opportunity to add a few essays extending the scope of the original group. The present book, then, includes the articles published in *Western Speech* and new contributions to that symposium.

It would have been most appropriate for Professor Wrage to have gathered a new set of essays to add to the old, and to share with us his thinking on what we have done and what we need yet to do. But we have been denied the opportunity of hearing from him again, as we have been denied further association with that generous and humane personality. We do him the greatest tribute by attempting to recapture the commitment to excellence that was his, not only as a scholar but as a man. In this spirit we dedicate the book to him.

Contents

Essays on Rhetorical Criticism

The Relation of
the Drama to Literature

BRANDER MATTHEWS

*Written just before the turn of the century, this essay expresses
the intellectual restiveness that was soon to characterize critics
of oratory who felt themselves hampered by the traditions and
influence of literary criticism. While primarily interested in
drama, Brander Matthews saw the common plight of the orator and dramatist whose works were evaluated by the literary
critic. The effect on the immediate audience of the qualities
of the spoken word and the expressive act was too often ignored by the literary critic in his preoccupation with the
beauty and permanence of the written word; but these elements are of vital concern to the speaker and performer. The
several arts, said Matthews, must be judged in terms of the
qualities peculiar to them, and this is no less true of oratory
and drama than of literature, painting, and sculpture.*

*Brander Matthews (1852–1929) was Professor of Literature
and Dramatic Literature, Columbia College, from 1892 to
1924. This article originally appeared in* Forum *(January
1898), pp. 630–640.*

The invention of printing and the extension of education
have given immense influence to the art of writing; and
hence has come about a tendency to judge the other arts by
the principles that govern literature. Rarely do we find a man
of letters who is not ready with his opinion of the picture in

the gallery, of the statue in the square, or of the play in the
theatre; and frequently his criticism is purely literary, being
supported by no special study of any other art than literature,
and being sustained by no familiarity with the principles of
painting, of sculpture, or of the drama. Generally, the man of
letters is lacking in appreciation of the individuality of each
of these several arts, of the essential qualities of each, peculiar to it alone, and therefore most relished by those who can
recognize this. In a picture, the man of letters sees chiefly the
story, the sentiment, the thought; he has little desire and little
knowledge to weigh the merits of technic, by which alone the
various arts are differentiated, one from the other.

The painters have long protested against any judgment of
their work in accordance with the principles of another art;
and at last they have succeeded in convincing the more open-
minded of us that what is of prime importance in a picture is
the way in which it is painted, and that its merely literary
merit is quite secondary. They are not unreasonable when
they insist that the chief duty of a picture is to represent the
visible world, not to point a moral or adorn a tale, and that in
the appreciation of a picture we must weigh first of all its
pictorial beauty. Nor are the sculptors asking too much, when
in a statue they want us to consider chiefly its plastic beauty.

Now, the orator and the dramatist ask for themselves
what has been granted the painter and the sculptor: they request that an oration or a drama shall be judged not as literature only, but also in accordance with the principles of its
own art. And here the literary critic is even less willing to
yield. He may acknowledge his own ignorance of perspective
and of pigments, of composition and of modelling; he may
confess that here the painter and the sculptor have him at a
disadvantage; but he is not ready to admit that he is not to
apply his own standards to the works of the orator and of the
dramatist. On the contrary, he maintains that the speech and
the play, if they belong to literature at all, are, by that very
fact, absolutely within the province of the literary critic. He
cannot see why that which the orator and the dramatist may

write is not to be read and criticised exactly as that which is
written by the novelist and the essayist and the poet. Indeed,
it is almost a misrepresentation of the literary critic's attitude
to suggest that he has need to maintain this position; for it is
rarely even hinted to him that he is not fully justified in employing the same tests in every department of literature.

Yet nothing ought to be clearer than the distinction between the written word and the spoken,—between the literature which is addressed to the eye alone and that which is
intended primarily for the ear and only secondarily for the
eye. It is the difference between words written once for all
and words first spoken and then written,—or at least written
so that they may be spoken. When this distinction is seized, it
follows that oral discourse is not necessarily to be measured
on the same scale as written discourse. It follows also that the
speech and the play may be very good indeed, each in its
kind, although they may fail to attain the standard of strictly
literary merit which we should demand in an essay, a story,
or a poem.

"Much of the ancient criticism of oratory," says Prof.
Jebb, "is tainted by a radical vice. The ancient critics too
often confound literary merit with oratorical merit. They
judge too much from the standpoint of the reader, and too
little from the standpoint of the hearer." For a just estimate
of the rank of a speaker, "the first thing necessary," the same
authority continues, "is an effort of imaginative sympathy.
We must not merely analyze his style; we must try to realize
the effect which some one of his speeches, as a whole, would
have made on a given audience in given circumstances." It is
this effort of imaginative sympathy which Schérer refused to
make, when he sought to show that Molière often wrote bad
French. Looking at some of the scenes of the great comic
dramatist from a purely literary standpoint, the critic found
many faults; but these blemishes to the eye, when the words
were read in the study, were, many of them, beauties to the
ear, when the words were spoken on the stage.

The dramatist and the orator are bound by many of the

same conditions; and one of these is inexorable: Each of them must please his immediate audience. The poet can appeal to posterity; but if the orator does not hold the attention of those whom he is addressing, his speech is a failure then and there, no matter how highly posterity may esteem it. The sermon accomplishes its purpose adequately, if it moves the congregation that listens to it; and so does a comedy, if it amuses the spectators that see it. If a speaker holds his hearers in the hollow of his hand while he is talking to them, and if he makes them thrill and throb with his words, then he has done what he set out to do, even if his words, when reproduced in cold type, fail absolutely to explain his success.

To affect his hearers is the first duty of the orator: to move his readers follows a long way after. That an oration should produce the same effect on both hearer and reader, is almost impossible: so competent a critic as Fox declared it to be quite impossible. When a certain speech was praised to him, he asked, "Does it read well?—because, be sure, if it does, it is a very bad speech." This is a hard saying. Indeed we need not hesitate to call it an overstatement, if we let our memory dwell on the oration of Demosthenes on the Crown, on Cicero's denunciation of Catiline, on Webster's reply to Hayne, and on Lincoln's Gettysburg address. But, like other overstatements, it may serve a useful purpose in putting into strong relief a side of the case which few of us see clearly. Lacordaire, a critic of eloquence as competent as Fox, is in substantial agreement with the latter. "The orator and the audience are two brothers," he declares, "who are born and who die the same day."

Perhaps cleverness is the final adjective to characterize Cicero; and certainly nothing could be cleverer than the skill with which the Roman rhetorician was able to meet the double demand on the orator,—if we may accept the suggestion of the late M. Goumy. The French critic maintained that the circumstances of the political situation in Rome made it physically impossible that Cicero could have delivered the diatribes against Catiline as they are preserved to us. They are too ornate to have been extemporized in the brief snatches of time at Cicero's command; and they are too long to have been endured by the impatient senate, restless at the crisis in the affairs of the republic. As the officer of state charged with the duty of discovering and putting down a conspiracy, Cicero no doubt made speeches to the senate; but what he actually said then—excellent as it was for its immediate purpose—can have been but a hasty outline of the successive orations as we have them now. Cicero was a born orator and a most accomplished master of the craft. No doubt the offhand speeches in which he reported the result of his detective work, and in which he solemnly set forth the awful dangers menacing the commonwealth,—no doubt, these speeches were vigorous and adroit, and aroused to enthusiasm those who heard them delivered by the impassioned consul. But, as soon as he had leisure, Cicero began to polish what he had said; and he did not leave it till he had made it what he would like to have said; thus combining the advantages of the impromptu with those of sober second thought,—the wit of the staircase, as the French call it.

As we are in the habit of recalling only the orations which are endowed with remarkable literary merit, we are naturally inclined to attribute to this literary merit their effectiveness when spoken, instead of seeking beneath the mere literature for the purely oratorical qualities which alone can account for their original success. To this day, we read with delight what Demosthenes said in Athens, what Cicero said in Rome, what Webster said in the Capitol, and what Lincoln said on the field of battle; but the Greek orator and the Roman and the two Americans were none of them thinking of us when they stood up to speak. Each of them was thinking of the men to whom he was speaking at that moment: he was addressing himself to those who were actually within sound of his voice and who were to be moved to action by the words he was about to speak. If he should accomplish his immediate purpose he would be amply satisfied; and if his sentences should also reverberate through time,—this would be but a surplusage of reward. The primary appeal was to those who were listening then; and the appeal to those who may read now is secondary and quite subsidiary.

To set up the immediate effect of the oration upon the audience as the chief test of the oratory may, to some, seem narrow. But, in so far as a man comes forward as a speaker, it is surely not unfair to judge him as a speaker. And the first duty of an orator is to hold the attention of those he is addressing,—or else why take the trouble of speaking at all? Why not ask leave to print and be done with it? Why go through the empty form of appealing to the ear, when the real intention is to appeal to the eye?

Some of the finest orations of Isocrates were apparently never delivered,—they seem, indeed, although strictly oratorical in form, to have been intended from the first to be read rather than recited; and when we remember how important a part in the development of Greek prose had been played by Greek oratory, we may even question whether Isocrates is fairly to be reckoned among the orators. But some of the finest orations of Burke might as well not have been spoken, for all the good their delivery accomplished. Burke's speeches are an inexhaustible storehouse of political wisdom from which succeeding generations will continue to help themselves. But, if we apply the test of immediate effectiveness upon the audience addressed, we are compelled to deny to Burke the rank of a great orator. It is not a question of the matter of his speech: it is a question of the manner of the speaker.

It is quite inconceivable that a great orator should put to flight those whom he wished to bring over to his way of thinking; yet this is what Burke did, not once only, but often. When he arose to address the Commons, the House emptied itself. He might "wind into his subject like a serpent"; but his fellow-members fled swiftly, to escape the fate of Laocoön. He was called the "dinner-bell"; and his friend Goldsmith has recorded that he

> still went on refining,
> And thought of convincing while they thought of dining.

Mr. John Morley judges that perhaps the greatest speech Burke ever made was that on conciliation with America,—

> the wisest in its temper, the most closely logical in its reasoning, the amplest in appropriate topics, the most generous and conciliatory in the substance of its appeals. Yet Erskine, who was in the House when this was delivered, said that it drove everybody away, including people who, when they came to read it, read it over and over again, and could hardly think of anything else.

In other words, Burke's greatest speech has the same merits as his "Letter to the Electors of Bristol"; and, for all the effect it produced, it might as well have been printed with no attempt at delivery. And here the kinship of Isocrates becomes evident; however superior the Irishman might be to the Greek in splendor and amplitude and penetration, they both of them lacked the first requisite of the orator. This condition precedent to triumph was possessed abundantly by Demosthenes and by Cicero, by Bossuet and by Webster,—men with whom it is not unfair to compare Burke.

It has been possessed also by many men of far inferior powers, lacking all things that Burke had, but having the one quality Burke was without. Who turns to Whitefield's sermons to-day for counsel or for comfort? But the size of the crowds that Whitefield attracted to hear him was limited only by the range of his voice. Who cares nowadays to shake the dust from off the five volumes of Sheridan's speeches ("edited by a constitutional friend")? And yet so potent was Sheridan's speech against Warren Hastings on the charge relative to the Princesses of Oude that an adjournment of the House was moved on the ground that it had left such an impression that no one could arrive at a determinate opinion; while Pitt and Grenville, after consultation, decided that Burke's speech on the Nabob of Arcot's debts was not worth answering.

This discussion of eloquence may seem to some a digression, or at least an excursus; but it is justified by the essential similarity of oratory and the drama, the two oral arts, standing on the same plane and to be judged by the same standards. For example, the position of Burke on the platform is not unlike that of Browning on the stage. We may see in Burke all the qualities of a great orator; but the fact remains that those whom he sought to influence by his voice did not listen to him eagerly. And we may discover in Browning the qualities of a great dramatist; but the fact remains that his plays were not able to hold their own in the theatre. And, in like manner, we may parallel the vogue of Whitefield as a preacher with that of playmakers like the authors of the "Two Orphans" and of the "Old Homestead," who are ready to rest content if they can entrance the playgoer, and who have no hope of attracting the attention of the reader.

It is possible to discover in more than one dramatist of high rank the same feeling of distrust for a play that reads well which Fox so frankly expressed for a speech that reads well; and it is easy to adduce instances where the dramatist, having won the kind of success he sought, has been satisfied with that, shrinking from a publication of his plays which would permit them to be tried by purely literary tests. John Marston, in the preface to his "Malcontent,"—which he printed only because a pirate had already sent forth an unauthorized text,—asserts that "only one thing affects me, to think that scenes invented merely to be spoken should be inforcively published to be read."

For the same reason, Molière was compelled to publish the "Précieuses Ridicules." He also wrote a preface, beginning it by saying that it is a strange thing for people to be printed against their wills. He does not affect to despise his comedy, for in these matters the public is the absolute judge; and even if he had had the worst possible opinion of his play before the performance, he ought now to believe that it is good for something, since so many people together have praised it. "But," he says,—and here is the pertinent passage,

—"but as a large part of the beauties which had been found in it depend on the gesture and on the tone of the voice, I thought it advisable that it should not be deprived of these ornaments; and I found the success which the play had had in the performance so great that I might leave it there." Thus we see that Molière, having composed at the same time the words of his piece and the stage business that set off and sustained the words, was wholly unwilling to present to the reading public his mere dialogue stripped naked. M. Coquelin, in his striking paper on Molière and Shakespeare, has remarked that each of these great dramatists had thrown his plays alive on the stage, and did not recognize them on paper. For the authors, "Tartuffe" and "Hamlet" existed "only before the footlights. It was only there that they felt their plays bone of their bone and flesh of their flesh." Both Shakespeare and Molière were accomplished men of letters; and both of them were also incomparable masters of the dramaturgic art; therefore, nobody knew better than they how much of its most valuable quality a play must inevitably lose in its transferal from the boards of the stage to the shelves of the library.

All the great dramatic critics have understood this; and they have tried steadily to cultivate the "imaginative sympathy" needful to enable them to see a play as it might appear on the stage, and to seek always under the flowing words for the solid framework of the acted drama. But great dramatic critics are strangely scarce: there are a scant half-dozen of them in all the history of literature. There were at least five great Greek dramatists; but Aristotle is the only critic of the acted drama worthy to be named with Aeschylus, Sophocles, Euripides, Aristophanes, and Menander. No great dramatic critic was a contemporary of the Elizabethan dramatists; and in the eighteenth century Lessing stands alone. The merely literary critic is rarely able to look for other than merely literary qualities. Even Charles Lamb, with all his liking for the theatre, collected specimens of the Elizabethan dramatists, which revealed them abundantly as poets and only casually as playwrights. The application of Lamb's method to the great-

est of all the Elizabethan dramatists might have preserved for
us more or less of the familiar quotations in Bartlett; but it
would never have suggested the possibility of a volume like
the "Tales from Shakespeare."

The true dramatic critic has discovered that the dramaturgic qualities are as special as the pictorial or the plastic,
and that, therefore, there is almost as much unfairness in
judging a play by the sole test of literature as in so judging a
picture or a statue. Indeed, to measure a drama by literature
alone is like trying to criticise a painting by a photograph
alone; and it is not the best painting that is most completely
represented by the camera.

M. Ferdinand Brunetière, tracing the epochs of the
French theatre, asserts unhesitatingly that a play is under no
obligation to be literary. "The drama," he declares, "can, if
need be, live on its own stock, on its own resources, relying
solely on its own means of expression." He explains that
while the epic, for example, and the ode must be literary, as a
condition of their existence, a comedy has no more call to be
literary than a sermon. This bold opinion of M. Brunetière's
is only an enlargement of an opinion of Aristotle's. To quote
from Prof. Butcher's admirable translation:—

> If you string together a set of speeches expressive of char-
> acter, and well finished in point of diction and thought, you
> will not produce the essential tragic effect nearly so well as
> with a play, which, however deficient in these respects, yet has
> a plot and artistically constructed incidents.

Thus we see that while literature may deal with words
alone, while it may be a matter of delicate verbal adjustment
only, the drama can get along without this refinement. The
literary merit of a play is in what the characters say; for that
is all that is spelt out in letters. The dramatic merit must be
sought beneath the surface: it is to be found in what the characters do, in what they feel, and in what they are. "Hence the
incidents and the plot are the end of tragedy; and the end is
the chief thing of all," said Aristotle. And again:—"Tragedy

is the imitation of an action, and of the agents, mainly with a view to the action."

After these quotations from two dramatic critics, let me quote also from two dramatic authors. The first is from the "Souvenirs" of M. Legouvé, perhaps best known to American theatre-goers as the collaborator of Scribe in the authorship of "Adrienne Lecouvreur." M. Legouvé tells us that

> the talent of the dramatist is a very singular and very special quality. It is not necessarily united to any other intellectual faculty. A man may have much wit, much learning, much literary skill, and yet be absolutely incapable of writing a play. I have seen men of real value and of high literary culture bring me dramas and comedies which seemed to be the work of a child. On the other hand, I have received from persons of no great intelligence plays in which was to be found a something nothing else can take the place of, a something which cannot be acquired, which is never lost, and which constitutes the dramatist.

And the second quotation is from the younger Dumas, from the illuminative preface which he prefixed to his "Père Prodigue." After asserting that the real dramatist is born, not made, Dumas declares that dramatic effect is sometimes so intangible that the spectator cannot find in the printed text of a play the point which charmed him in its performance, and which was due perhaps to "a word, a look, a gesture, a silence, a purely atmospheric combination." And then he goes on to say that "a man of no value as a thinker, as a moralist, as a philosopher, as a writer, may be a man of the first order as a dramatic author"; and, "on the other hand, for a thinker, a writer, a philosopher, to be listened to upon the stage, he must indispensably be provided with the special qualities of the man who has no other value. In short, to be a master in this art, one must be also skilled in this craft."

The history of the drama has a long list of more or less forgotten playwrights, skilled in the craft of the theatre, cunning in stage-effect, and owning no other superiority. But this dramaturgic faculty, which they had as a sole possession, was also the gift of all the great dramatists, who had this in addition to their poetry, their philosophy, their psychology. No intricate plot of Scribe's is more adroitly contrived than the "Oedipus" of Sophocles; and no melodrama of Kotzebue's is more artfully constructed than the "Othello" of Shakespeare. Vision and insight Sophocles and Shakespeare had, as well as subtlety and power,—things unsuspected by the writers of the "Ladies' Battle" and of the "Stranger." But the greatness of Shakespeare and Sophocles as dramatists was due, first of all, to that same gift of playmaking which was the whole of Scribe's possession and the whole of Kotzebue's.

It matters not how beautiful a building may be, if its structure be feeble and faulty; for then it can be neither useful nor durable. Strength must precede grace; and the dramatic poet must begin by being a practical playwright, just as an architect must master construction. Whenever a poet denies this obligation, and shrinks from due apprenticeship to stagecraft, he surrenders his chance of being a dramatist. The stage of their own times is the platform upon which the real dramatists have always found themselves at home. Euripides and Calderon and Corneille did not retire into an ivory tower: they brought out plays to please the broad public. There is no more patent absurdity than the play that is not intended to be played,—the closet-drama, as it is called.

This unactable drama of lofty poetic pretence is largely a development of our own day, although it may find a doubtful ancestor in the tragedy of Seneca. The Roman rhetorician did not intend his pieces to be performed; and this is fortunate for him, as the fate is not doubtful of plays in which the deed is forever sacrificed to the word, and in which the heartfelt cry is suppressed in favor of the elaborated antithesis. Whether Browning and Tennyson and Swinburne had it in them to be dramatists, nobody knows; but nobody can deny that they are not dramatists as were Goethe and Schiller, as are Ibsen and Hauptmann. However various their qualifications, they fail to reveal the most important of all—the possession of sufficient stagecraft to make the performance of their plays profitable.

It is in this ability to hold the attention of an average audience of their own contemporaries that the inspired dramatists stand side by side with the uninspired playmakers. Poets they are, but, first of all, theatre-poets, in the apt German phrase. Even to-day, despite the gulf of two thousand years that yawns between us and the civilization of Greece, we are gripped by the inexorable action as the awful fate of *Oedipus* is unrolled before us in the playhouse, and we are dissolved in pity. And as for the sad story of *Hamlet,* were that performed in an asylum for the deaf and dumb, there would be no fear that the interest of the spectators would flag. There is that in "Hamlet" which the deaf would fail to get; and no doubt this is what gives the play its significance; but what they could take in by the eye alone would reward them amply for the effort. By whom was it first said that the skeleton of a good play was always a pantomime? And whoever has had the pleasure of seeing "L'Enfant Prodigue" has had proof positive that the drama can exist without even the elements of literature; for here was a play that made us laugh and made us cry, with never a word spoken.

The dramatists themselves have never had any doubts as to the relative importance of the theatrical and the literary elements in a play. To them, the skeleton of action is everything; and nothing, the verbal epidermis. In the preface to the "Mariage de Figaro," Beaumarchais assures us that, when he had mastered the subject of a play, he saw the characters before him. "What they will say, I don't know: it is what they are going to do that interests me." And Racine is recorded to have told a friend that a new tragedy of his was nearly completed,—as he had only to write it. Here, in Beaumarchais and in Racine, we see an incipient contempt for mere literature that came to a head in the advertisement of a New York theatre a few years ago, wherein it was proclaimed, as one of the elements of attraction of a certain more or less comic play, that it was "without literary merit."

A rough-and-tumble farce, hastily knocked together by a variety-show performer, to satirize rudely some folly of the moment, is of more importance in the actual development of the drama than can be any string of soliloquies and dialogues, however poetic or polished these may be. The farce that pleases the people has in it the root of the matter: here is the germ of the real thing; while the drama for the closet lingers lifeless and inert on the shelves of the library. The influence of the unpretending popular play—the folk-theatre, as one might call it—is far deeper and wider than most historians of literature have perceived. The beginnings of Molière's comedy must be sought in the French farces and in the Italian improvisations of his boyhood; and no one has yet worked out the exact indebtedness of Victor Hugo and the elder Dumas to Pixérécourt and Ducange and the other melodramatists of the boulevard-theatres, whose labors made the path straight for the Romanticists.

The reason why this folk-theatre was soon forgotten is simply because it lacked literature. Its merits were not only primarily theatrical; they were wholly theatrical. These plays were actable, but they were not readable; and when they ceased to be acted, they disappeared into darkness. The instant that they were crowded off the stage, they fell sheer into oblivion. The success of a play, be it tragedy or comedy, depends upon its fitness for the playhouse and for the players of its own time; but the survival of a play depends on its literary quality. Only literature is permanent. As the younger Dumas goes on to say, in the preface from which I have already quoted,

> a dramatic work should always be written as though it was only to be read. The performance is only a reading aloud by several persons for the benefit of those who will not or cannot read. It is through those who go to the theatre that the work succeeds; and it is by those who do not go that it subsists. The spectator gives it vogue; and the reader makes it durable.

Upon this side of the discussion there is no need to dwell. Nobody disputes that dramatic literature must be literature, although there are not a few who do not insist that it must be dramatic. The great dramatists have accepted the double obligation; and they have always recognized that the stage of the theatre, and not the desk of the library, is the true proving-room. This double obligation it is that makes the drama so difficult an art,—perhaps, indeed, the most difficult of all the arts.

Public Address as
Intellectual Revelation

JOSEPH L. BLAU

"In a word," says Joseph Blau, "it is the province of the philosophic critic of public address to weigh the credibility of its intellectual revelations." Such weighing requires that the critic search out the philosophic assumptions on which the speech is based, for only then can he fully appreciate the implications of the propositions presented—the further commitments their acceptance implies.

Joseph L. Blau is Professor of Philosophy and Religion at Columbia University. His article is reprinted from the original Western Speech *symposium.*

In esthetics and in the philosophy of criticism, as well as in ethical theory and other value disciplines where the trend is more often recognized, the tendency of much that has been written during the past quarter of a century has been to question whether there is "meaning," that is, an intellectual component, in the arts, beside their obvious and undenied "expressive" or "emotive" component. These discussions have been carried on under the spur of a far more careful and sophisticated analysis of "the meaning of 'meaning'" than had prevailed before Ogden and Richards wrote their influential book under that title. One of the dominant schools of thought has tended to limit the significant use of the term "meaning" to assertory judgments to which we can ascribe truth or falsity in terms of criteria fixed by reference to the sort of propositions that make up the positive sciences. Other philosophic writers who resist this more precise delimitation of "meaning," especially those who are concerned with the analysis of the work of art rather than with the analysis of statements about works of art, with ethical behavior rather than with statements about ethical behavior, with religious beliefs and practices rather than with statements about religious beliefs and practices, have attempted to maintain that non-referential uses of language, especially symbolic uses, are on the same plane of philosophic respectability as the referential uses so honorifically exalted by their opponents.

It is not my intention here to contribute to the technical aspect of this discussion, nor do I intend to take one side or the other in the dispute. I am concerned, rather, to suggest an art form, the study of which may prove particularly fruitful both for professional philosophers and for a paradigmatic "well-educated man." It seems to me unfortunate that in many of the discussions to which reference has been made, illustrative materials are sought in extreme forms of expression—mathematical or physical statements, on the one hand, and on the other, musical compositions or non-objective paintings. Meantime, a fertile field for study exists in public address which, in most instances, involves both an intellectual and an emotive component. More than in any other art form, save possibly some dramatic poetry, public address demands the marriage of intellect and emotion. As in other marriages, much can happen in public address to mar perfect felicity. Overattention to intellectual content may produce a logical masterpiece to which no one can listen. Overattention to emotional content may lead to dangerous forms of demagoguery. Blended in proper proportions, intellect and emotion can make of public address one of the most stimulating and effective methods of influencing people and thereby determining the course of public policy. And if you will concede a social definition of liberty—that liberty is the opportu-

nity for the individual to influence society by taking a part in
the formulation of public policy—then it is clear that in a
democracy whose object is "to insure liberty to all the people," public address is inevitably an important instrument of
liberty.

Beyond this general statement suggesting the place of
public address in a democratic social philosophy, a philosophic critic finds himself doubly drawn to public address as
food for his thought. In the first place, there is an explicit
speculative content that forms public address; and, in the second place, there is an implicit and often unconscious ground-
work of philosophic views that underlies the thought of each
speaker. The philosophic critic of public address must develop tools and techniques for the exploration, explication,
and elucidation of both the expressed and the implied
philosophic views. These techniques must be philosophic;
their use by the critic can supplement but cannot replace the
use of the tools of rhetorical study, historical evaluation and
psychological analysis. Perhaps a better way to say this is that
the philosophic criticism of public address is of little value
unless the philosophic critic has more than a layman's knowledge of rhetoric, history, and psychology. But he cannot stop
with this, or his work is rhetorical, historical, psychological
criticism. Philosophic criticism must unearth the presupposi-
tions and assumptions on which the public address is based
by a reconstruction of the system of general propositions,
acknowledged or not, that justifies the speaker's text. These
general propositions must then be examined for their internal
logical consistency as well as for their place in the history of
ideas. Their consequences beyond those presented in the text
must be elaborated, again by the application of rigorous logic.
In a word, it is the province of the philosophic critic of public
address to weigh the credibility of its intellectual revelations.

Explicitly expressed philosophic views do not present the
critic with many difficulties. A speaker sets out to say something and, well or ill, say it he does. What he says is usually
readily recognizable to one habituated to philosophic dis-

course. His statements can be set, roughly, within one of the traditional patterns of thought current in his age. The further implications of what he says can be worked out. In fairness to the speaker these ulterior implications should be analyzed in terms of a logic that he would accept; in practice this requirement is seldom observed. Ideally, it should ultimately be possible for the philosophic critic to expound the total worldview of a good, philosophic public speaker on the basis of a typical sample of his better work, a sample in which there is a proper blending of intellect and emotion.

So, for example, when George Santayana in 1933, during the celebration of the tercentenary of the birth of Spinoza, delivered an address entitled "Ultimate Religion," his text conveyed clearly the deep emotion with which it was freighted. His language was that of the platform, not that of the study. The prose in which Santayana expressed his impassioned thought soared at the conclusion of the address toward the loftiest poetry:

> . . . when power takes on the form of life, and begins to circle about and pursue some type of perfection, spirit in us necessarily loves these perfections, since spirit is aspiration become conscious, and they are the goals of life: and insofar as any of these goals of life can be defined or attained anywhere, even if only in prophetic fancy, they become glory, or become beauty, and spirit in us necessarily worships them: not the troubled glories and brief perfections of this world only, but rather that desired perfection, that eternal beauty, which lies sealed in the heart of each living thing.

Surely this passage compares favorably with any passage in the literature of public address for its rhetorical and emotive qualities. Yet it is not difficult to read back from it the entire systematic structure of what has been called Santayana's "poetic naturalism" with its view that matter (here "power") is the ultimate basis on which life and mind and spirit are totally dependent, that "spirit" and "the spiritual life" are forms of imaginative play in the foreground of a universe whose firm and fixed scenery is matter and material force.

In practice there are usually certain well-defined limits to what the critic can make of one speech, especially by a non-philosopher. A sermon, for example, may give a clear basis for expounding the cosmology, the psychology, and the ethical theory of the speaker, as well as his theology. Many of the sermons of Jonathan Edwards, William Ellery Channing, Theodore Parker, and other first-rate American religious leaders yield to this much analysis. Indeed, Edwards' sermon, "A Divine and Supernatural Light immediately imparted to the soul by the spirit of God" (1734), contains in essence the entire psychological and epistemological structure later to be given systematic expression in the preacher's *Treatise concerning Religious Affections* (1746). In the sermon Edwards presents his device of postulating a "supernatural sense" as the epistemological counterpart of the Calvinist doctrine of the infusion of divine grace, a device by means of which he brought this theology into accord with John Locke's sensationalistic psychology. Again, it is possible to reconstruct the entire critical theology of Theodore Parker in its maturest form from the four sermons he preached in 1858 in the yearly meeting of the Progressive Friends at Longwood (Pa.). Some of Horace Bushnell's sermons, notably those on "Christian Nurture" (1847), make positive and original contributions to philosophical theology with what was at that time a radical restatement of the doctrine of human nature.

Furthermore, a breakdown of the rhetorical structure of a sermon may tell us much about the logic in which the preacher was schooled. Perry Miller has demonstrated the importance of Ramist logic to the Puritan divines, and Babette M. Levy's study of preaching in the first half century of New England has drawn extremely interesting ideological conclusions from a careful and detailed rhetorical study. Yet it is only in rare and exceptional cases, at critical periods in the relation of church and state or of theology and science, that a sermon will reveal much of the social philosophy or of the philosophy of science held by the preacher. A most unusual instance, possibly the most revealing single sermon in the entire history of American preaching, is Urian Oakes' Artillery Election Sermon at Cambridge, September 10, 1677, printed at Boston in 1682 under the title "The Soveraign Efficacy of Divine Providence," which develops a philosophy of science in terms of primary and secondary causation in order to make a theologico-political point in one of the controversies then raging in New England. Some of the sermons of the Revolutionary era, too, as collected in Thornton's *Pulpit of the American Revolution,* tell us as much about the preachers' political and social thought as they do about their theology. A recent dissertation, at Teachers College, Columbia University, by Martha Counts, has made systematic use of election sermons in the New England colonies to study the political and social views of the clergy through the eighteenth century. Again, many sermons delivered during the controversies over the religious consequences of geological and biological studies during the nineteenth century do give voice to their authors' philosophies of science. More recently, some of the sermons preached by, for example, John Haynes Holmes in the course of the renewal of the evolutionary controversy in the 1920s present a fairly clear statement of Holmes' views on philosophy of science. These are exceptional cases; for the most part, except in critical eras, we are forced to extrapolate by analogy with some philosophic systems that are in accord with the preacher's views as far as we know them directly. But we must bear in mind, as so many have since the elections of 1948, the perils of extrapolation.

Similarly, a political address, whatever it may tell of the political and economic thought of its author and, perhaps, of his ethics and of his logical background, is not likely to tell us much about the politician's theological views, unless we are willing to accept as theological views the polite references to God and the men of the cloth inserted for the benefit of the "folks-back-home." A rare case of a most interesting systematic philosophy implied in an address whose intent was basi-

cally political is the transcendental idealism that emerges into
social and political expression in Job Durfee's "The Influence
of Scientific Discovery and Invention on Social and Political
Progress" (1843). This speech, however, though it was political in intent, was delivered before the Phi Beta Kappa Society of Brown University, rather than a political audience.
Even the great political addresses of, for example, the Lincoln-Douglas debates lack meat when studied philosophically. It is possible for us to supply the deficiency in terms
that seem to us to be consistent with the views that the
speaker has expressed, but we do this at the risk of inaccu-
rately representing the speaker's thought.

Regardless of risk, however, we must extend the limits in
the way suggested if our purpose is serious, if we are not just
playing intellectual games with ourselves. For our primary
purpose in carrying out this examination of the views of
preacher or politician or any other public speaker is to determine whether we are going to accept the position he is pre-
senting. How can we know whether to accept the preacher's
doctrine of God or the politician's doctrine of the state until
we know to what other doctrines we are committing ourselves by this acceptance? If we are to live a "life of reason,"
at least to the extent that we attempt to maintain consistency
in our own views, we must examine the consequences for our
total belief in any one doctrine. We may find that, in isolation
from the rest of our thinking, a particular theory of the state,
expressed in a political address, is most attractive; we may
also wish to accept a particular doctrine of the nature of God
that we have heard in a sermon. Further philosophic consideration may show us that the appealing doctrine of the state
has theological implications that conflict with the equally appealing doctrine of the nature of God. Furthermore, either of
these doctrines or their combination may have psychological
consequences or entail certain doctrines of the nature and
scope of human knowledge that we are not prepared to
accept.

It is important for the point that is being made here for us to remember that interdependence is as characteristic of ideas as it is of human beings. For this reason, we must learn never to consider accepting an idea without examining the train of ideas it brings with it. We must be prepared to reconstruct the entire system involved in any idea that seems on first hearing to be worthy of our belief. To do this, we must, in examining public address philosophically, dare to go beyond the direct evidence, trusting our skill in analysis to bring us to accurate conclusions. How fortunate we are, then, when we find the unusual sermon, political oration, or other address which is so explicit that it makes this leap into the dark unnecessary. Much more often we find fuller revelation in academic or semi-academic addresses. Phi Beta Kappa orators, speakers before learned societies, and lecturers on foundations or endowments supply the finest grist for the mill of philosophic criticism. Unfortunately such addresses comprise but a small fragment of the whole order; for the most part, we are on our own.

Another and often a far more exacting task of the philosophic critic of public address is the exploration of the often unconscious underlying positions of the speaker. This is in a literal sense a concern for the speaker's assumptions, for what the speaker takes for granted. In most cases, the point is not merely that the speaker fails to defend these positions by argument or evidence; he often does not even realize that there is anything that needs defense. He may never put into words his unargued, undefended substructure of ideas; it may seem to him too obviously "self-evident" to mention. Yet it may well condition every later thing that he says. So, in the misnamed Middle Ages, no speaker would have thought it necessary to begin an address by saying "I am certain that the earth is flat." Yet a moment's reflection will suffice to convince us that just such an assumption as this may very well have colored his entire speech and have been the logical foundation of his every other proposition. Nor, again, would the post-Newtonian counterpart of our hypothetical medieval speaker bother to tell his audience of his belief in the order and regularity of nature. A large part of the enterprise of the philosophic critic of public address consists in bringing to light and examining in the context of present-day knowledge just such foundational assumptions as these.

These assumptions come into the minds of public speakers from a variety of sources. Some are prejudices imbibed with mothers' milk; most of the assumptions which divide the world into "our" kind and "the other" kind, "insiders" and "outsiders," are acquired early in life. Some are instilled in the course of early religious training. Others represent local, regional or national idiosyncracies, family traditions, or reflections of a critical period in the experience of a group. Broadly speaking, it is possible to describe all these sources as non-philosophic. This creates a major difficulty for the philosophic critic of public address. One of his primary problems is to determine the influence of non-philosophic sources of unexpressed assumptions upon the speakers' speculative and philosophic world-views. To complicate the matter even further, these non-philosophic sources do not necessarily yield fruit after their own kind; they do not necessarily give rise to beliefs of only one order, of a self-consistent order. Family traditions may be the source of political assumptions and need not be the source of assumptions about the family. Economic assumptions or social prejudices may be the result of religious training. An inconsistency at the crown of a speaker's thought is not necessarily an indication of faulty thinking; it may be the belated result of two inconsistent and unreconciled assumptions followed independently to their logical conclusions. For reasons such as these it may be an extremely complex and difficult task for the critic to unearth and in some measure to structure the basic assumptions of a speaker. Yet this, too, must be done if we are to make sense out of what the speaker has to say.

The task of the public speaker in a majority of cases is to

try to influence others—among them ourselves—to join in his way of regarding issues. He has two fundamental appeals at his command: one emotional, the other intellectual. For best results, these two appeals must be well-blended, though the exact proportions of the blend will differ from speaker to speaker. The mechanism by which the emotional appeal is made effective is one which the psychologist can best analyze. Perhaps the psychologist is also the person to tell how the appeal to the intellect can best be engineered. But it seems that the listener has a responsibility here because the effectiveness of the intellectual appeal is at least as much under his control as under the speaker's. Our responses to an emotional appeal may be very largely involuntary; we cannot admit that this is also the case with respect to our responses to an intellectual appeal.

It has recently been pointed out by a number of writers who have been impressed with the results of advertising campaigns and public relations build-ups that men can be led to a course that is not in their best interests by skillful manipulation of the emotional content of public address. This seems to be an exaggeration; men may be so led in matters of little moment, but in matters of major importance we are convinced that this cannot be done. Still the statement itself points to an obligation, especially for educators. To offset such a manipulative conception of public address, we must find ways to strengthen the weapon of reason in the arsenal of democracy. "Truth is great and will prevail," but only if an instrument for detecting truth, an intellectual Geiger counter, is made available to men by their education. We conceive the philosophic criticism of public address to be such an instrument.

Philosophic criticism of public address is the careful study of the foundations and conclusions of the intellectual appeal of the speaker in the attempt to assure ourselves of the validity, the consistency and the desirability of the conclusions toward which the speaker is drawing our minds.

Were an instrument of this sort widely available to the audience for public address in America, it could be a potent force for elevating the standards of public discourse. Were there a critical audience, our speakers would be compelled to recognize that public address is an important form of intellectual revelation and not a mere "performance."

The Criticism of Rhetoric
and the Act of Communication

JAMES T. BOULTON

Rhetorical criticism "must examine the nature of the act of communication in persuasive discourse, in all its complexity and ramifications." Professor Boulton fully recognizes the indispensable nature of the historical approach in criticism, but his interest here is in the use of language—in the broadest sense of the term—in the situation. Analysis of the language of persuasive discourse takes us beyond the "formal or structural features" to idiom, imagery, and whatever other qualities contribute to the "total rhetorical experience."

James T. Boulton is Professor of English Literature at Nottingham University. His article is printed here for the first time.

An extract from a recent essay by Raymond Williams provides a valuable starting point:

One of the marks of a conservative society is that it regards style as an absolute. A style of writing and speaking is judged as a question of manners, and appreciation of this style as a question of taste. In important literary criticism, since the time of Coleridge, this merely conventional judgment has in fact been set aside: style is not an abstract quality, but is inseparable from the substance of the ideas and feelings expressed. In modern communication theory, a new dimension has been added: style is also inseparable from the precise relationship, whether explicit or assumed, between a writer or speaker and his expected reader or audience. This is never a mechanical relationship; the ordinary formula for communication—"who says what to whom with what effect?"—characteristically neglects the real sources of communication. A more adequate formula—would be *"why does* who say what to whom with what effect?"* It is clear, also, that the precise relationship, in any act of communication, is not finally separable from the substantial ideas and feelings. In almost all speech and writing, this substance includes, though often unconsciously, the real relationship, of the writer or speaker and other men.

It is remarkable how often, in literary criticism but especially in ephemeral commentary, the mechanical version of style as an abstract quality, supported of course by the unnoticed conventions and traditions of particular groups, is still in practice assumed. But when the writing or speaking in question is not literary, the assumption is almost universal. Style is regarded as a decoration, a merely tasteful or mannered addition to substance, even in politics, where the kind of experience being drawn on and the version of other men indicated by a particular way of talking to them, are not only substantial but are even crucial to the precise nature of a political act.[1]

In this statement Williams stresses the central and complex nature of the relationship that exists between a writer or speaker and his audience whenever an act of communication takes place. He rightly emphasizes that, whatever the subject or occasion of the discourse, criticism cannot properly function unless this relationship is explored. He might also have explicitly affirmed the importance of "situation," the context in which communication is established, of which both writer and audience are a part, and on which they exert influence. In the case of private correspondence the situation will be personal and intimate; on the other hand it may be public, as with Burke's speeches on Economical Reform or Conciliation with America, but created by specific events which called for equally specific action; or yet again, it may have the complexity of the political or religious controversies which gave rise, for example, to Paine's *Rights of Man* or Newman's *Apologia pro Vita Sua*. In these last instances the situation is fluid and, though having a recognizable dialectical center, is constantly being reshaped by the efforts of each participant. None of these categories is exclusive—clearly Burke's response to the parliamentary situation was not only to the words on the order paper but also to what previous speakers in the debate had made of them; Milton in his *Areopagitica* does not confine his attention to the licensing system but dilates on the broad issues of the nation's moral and political health. Nevertheless, in each case the situation is a decisive factor. Unless we explore it fully we cannot answer Williams' question, *"why does* who say what to whom?"

The final words in his question—"with what effect?"—form a relevant though a potentially hazardous criterion unless certain safeguards are defined. Hitler's speeches had massive effect; other demagogues have been highly successful in persuading their audiences to action of a more or less desirable kind; whereas several speeches by Fox or Burke, recognized by posterity as masterly orations, were ineffectual. Defoe's *Shortest-Way with the Dissenters* produced, initially at any rate, the reverse of the effect aimed at. Indeed if Williams' question regarding "effect" is to prompt qualitative judgments and not merely description, it needs delicate handling. Perhaps we should be honest enough to state that effect is sometimes not measurable, that it may not be a mark of oratorical or literary excellence, and that in most cases it should be judged in the long term: what degree of permanent interest or pleasure has the discourse given to mankind, whether or not they were part of the original audience? By this measure we recognize the excellence of Burke's speeches and the shoddiness of Hitler's.

From what has been said so far it might appear superficially that the business of the rhetorical critic is exhausting but relatively straightforward: establish all the discoverable facts about the situation, audience and speaker or writer, and then decide "why does who say what to whom." If this were true then the historical or "extrinsic" critic might appear supreme, his timorous trust in verifiable facts justified. Certainly without the information he can supply, rhetorical criticism cannot function satisfactorily. For example, unless the original situation is thoroughly known, one can make the wrong assumptions about a writer's or speaker's purpose, misunderstand his tone of voice, misinterpret his allusions, or be ignorant of extrinsic circumstances which were of cardinal importance in shaping his discourse. Information which prevents such blunders is vital; it provides a foundation for the critical act; but it must not be confused with the superstructure to be built on it. Extrinsic criticism by itself is barren; in association with the intrinsic it is essential. The ideal critic—of rhetorical as of all literary discourse—must concern himself not only with the "facts" alluded to, but also with the orator's primary meaning and the subtle suggestiveness communicated by his tone; the patterns of thought and argument which sometimes reveal themselves in clearly definable ways but sometimes in a manner of which the speaker himself may have been only dimly aware; his idiom and imagery; his sense of the rhythm and sound of language; and with his understanding of the character—in the fullest sense—of his intended audience. This is, of course, merely to hint at the kind of approach that would seem normal to a critic of "literature"; only—as Williams remarks—where "the writing or speaking in question is not literary," but rather "political" or in some sense an "occasional" act of public communication, do these critical methods unaccountably seem to some to be out of place or irrelevant.

A single question will illustrate this general reluctance to grapple with the critical issues raised by publications which, in their day, were of vital consequence to their authors and public, and which remain of continuing interest. Wilkes' *North Briton* No. 45 is mentioned countless times in studies of the eighteenth century: how often has it been examined by a rhetorical critic? It surely is important to decide how far governmental reaction to the "No. 45" can be attributed to extrinsic reasons—fear of the power of the press, Wilkes' public "image," or a nervous administration—and how far the author's literary manner was responsible. The question has obvious significance for the historian, but the rhetorical critic must clearly be involved in resolving it. One approach open to him might be to compare Wilkes' paper with Defoe's *Legion's Memorial*. The work of experienced journalists and political writers, both pieces proclaim "the spirit of liberty"; both are addressed partly to Parliament, partly to the general public; both are threatening and defiant—*"Englishmen* are no more to be Slaves to *Parliaments,* than to a King" (Defoe) might be from either publication; both protest against the encroachment on "the ancient liberties of this kingdom"; and both achieved an effect that can in part be assessed. Yet there are differences between them, the examination of which would help to define the essential character of both publications. To select one point of similarity which also points to an important distinction, both pieces end with a quotation:

WILKES: The Prerogative of the Crown is to exert the Constitutional powers entrusted to it in a way not of blind favour and partiality, but of wisdom and judgment. This is the spirit of our Constitution. The people, too, have their prerogative, and I hope the fine words of Dryden will be engraven on our hearts:
Freedom is the English subject's Prerogative.

DEFOE: Thus, *Gentlemen,* you have your Duty laid before you, which it is hoped you will think of; but if you continue to neglect it, you may expect to be treated according to the Resentments of an *injur'd Nation; for Englishmen* are no more to be Slaves to *Parliaments,* than to a King.
Our Name is Legion, and we are many.

Both writers sought an impressive close which would be memorable, easily quoted by their supporters. Wilkes chose a

high-sounding line relevant to his subject—though selecting
it, oddly enough, from Dryden's "Poem Sacred to the Happy
Memory of King Charles II" and, perhaps to avoid ambiguity, omitting Dryden's penultimate word, "sole"—whereas
Defoe's choice was the familiar biblical sentence. The latter is
the more effective, not only because it was better known, but
also because it confirms the feeling given by the whole *Memorial* that this is no casual remonstrance; rather is it the
voice of a mission undertaken in the name of the whole nation. As a result the well-known quotation is transformed
from a cliché into a statement of menacing power. Wilkes,
for his part, protests too stridently and volubly throughout his
paper that he is the mouthpiece of the whole people; he makes
overt threats; his anger is on the surface and superlatives
abound; and he gives the impression of a man barely in control of his prose medium. The consequence is that the words
from Dryden, expressed with the formality of verse and lacking the extreme intensity of Wilkes' own language, come as
an anticlimax. They do not sustain the vehemence of the preceding paragraphs; they are not so finely phrased as to be
inevitably remembered; indeed one suspects that they were
the choice of a demagogue in search of dignity. But it is a
false dignity.

Much more could be added about the famous *North
Briton* if space allowed; all I have done is to begin to place it
critically. However, some tentative conclusions can be suggested. While men of all cultural classes would undoubtedly
read Wilkes out of a delight in scandal or in swingeing attacks
on the Ministry, few outside the "mob" (to use Fielding's
nonsocial term) [2] would be influenced by him. Stylistic analysis suggests that Wilkes fell foul of the government for extrinsic as much as intrinsic reasons; his was a bombastic
rather than a fundamental threat; he was in fact a demagogue
who was dangerous because of his appeal to men discon-
tented from other causes.

If, then, rhetorical criticism is to be fully effective it must
examine the nature of the act of communication in persuasive

discourse, in all its complexity and ramifications. To achieve this end the skills of the literary critic must, ideally, be associated with those of the historian of politics, culture, and society, the philosopher, and the specialist in the particular field of a specific speech or writing. The scope for joint and fruitful endeavor is unlimited. There is, for example, a vast opportunity for collaborative inquiry into what might be called the "image" of George III. How much was it the result of the King's own maneuverings and how much of the political situation of which he was only a part? To what extent was it created by political writers, satirists, and orators: Wilkes, Junius, Pindar, or Burke? To what extent was Byron's attitude to George in "The Vision of Judgment" or Fonblanque's in the *Examiner* generally shared? Did such writers merely perpetuate the image which had been previously established? Answers to such questions would certainly affect our view of the writers mentioned; they would increase our understanding of the reign; and central to much of the inquiry would be the work of the rhetorical critic. Whenever men publicly communicate with their fellows in an effort to secure *persuasion,* whether by the spoken or written word, he should feel involved.

Newman's *Apologia* is a case in point. It seems fairly simple, in answer to Williams' question, "why does who say what . . . ?", to reply that Newman wished to justify his own course of action and to refute Kingsley's charges against him. It can be shown that for this purpose Newman produces a narrative of his spiritual and intellectual development; he gives evidence of the stages by which he accepted the superior claims of Roman Catholicism; and he undoubtedly tries to convince the reader of the propriety of his final choice. But to say this is certainly not to account for the contemporary or the permanent impact made by the *Apologia*. It is a persuasive work of a subtle kind; it requires all the skill of the rhetorical critic to assess it. He will not wholly succeed alone; the theologian and historian should also be involved, but primarily the challenge is his.

Though, for instance, Newman claimed that he wishes "simply to state facts," his tone at the outset is immensely important:

> It is not at all pleasant for me to be egotistical; nor to be criticized for being so. It is not pleasant to reveal to high and low, young and old, what has gone on within me from my early years. It is not pleasant to be giving to every shallow or flippant disputant the advantage over me of knowing my most private thoughts. . . .

At once the reader is induced to participate in the self-analysis of a man reluctantly compelled to publicize "the intercourse between [himself] and [his] Maker"; compelled to do so by Kingsley who "has no personal knowledge of [him] to set right his misconceptions," and whom Newman has never seen. The reader, then, is to obtain insights not available to Newman's adversary, and immediately an intimate relationship is established between writer and audience. Again, when Newman begins his account of the influences affecting him in his earlier years—ranging from Paine and the Gothic novelists to Scott and the Romantic poets—he is assuring his readers that there is common ground between them, that— initially at any rate—the *Apologia* will not cover territory completely foreign to them. But these ordinary and diverse experiences cumulatively prove to be part of the inescapable forces which direct Newman towards the decision taken on October 8, 1845. The inevitability of this development is his central theme; that it involves experiences shared with Newman's readers carries implications too plain to be missed. Associated with this theme are the numerous hints that Newman felt himself an agent under the direction of a ruling Providence; they not only dignify his career but also undermine the kind of criticism that impugned the honesty of his final decision; and cumulatively they win the reader's assent. To further strengthen this theme, Newman gives the impression of extreme urgency. He uses, for example, a variety of prose media—narrative, sermons, letters, quotations from pamphlets, or snatches of direct conversation—all, taken together, communicating the excitement of a mind recollecting significant evidence. The inference is that an unlimited reservoir of evidence existed, all of it bearing on the crucial decision. Then there is the vivid imagery suggesting action that was courageous, continuous, or urgent: Hurrell Froude was "a bold rider, as on horseback, so also in his speculations"; the trial to be made of the English Church was "like proving cannon"; or the frequently recurring sea imagery, instinct with unceasing and irresistible energy. Such qualities reinforce on the level of suggestion or "submerged" persuasiveness what is urged on the surface by logical argument: that Newman was right to reject a "paper system" in favor of a religion which "would *work*."

What is implied by this glance at the *Apologia* is that the rhetorical critic cannot remain satisfied with an analysis of purely formal or structural features; he must—if he is to account for other, less tangible but permanently affecting characteristics—examine what might be called the "imaginative logic" of a work. Rhetorical discourse, operating on two main levels—the logical and argumentative, and the imaginative or emotive—provides for the listener or reader an experience that is highly complex and not solely intellectual. Newman does not merely refute Kingsley or prove through argument the rightness of his secession; by means touched on earlier, he communicates a wide range of emotions, imaginative insights, a sense of personal dignity and honesty, and a sympathetic personality, all of which are combined with intellectual penetration to form a total rhetorical experience. Similarly Burke, in his speech on Fox's East India Bill, not only logically refutes the objections to the measure, but also conveys his revulsion from certain practices and values, a sense of his own moral and emotional maturity, and his imaginative and sympathetic understanding, which in sum both communicate and affirm a view of what is important in all human dealings. It is

precisely these characteristics which are largely inaccessible
to an analysis of the purely formal elements in his speech.

What can be achieved by examining such elements is
shown by Professor John L. Mahoney.[3] He demonstrates the
care with which Burke employs "a calm, insinuating exor-
dium" to reduce the tension in the Commons and to quiet the
hostility to Fox's Bill. A brief "narration" follows, allowing
the speaker to clarify the state of the question at issue and to
remove "the clouds of ignorance and of prejudice." This is
followed, in its turn, by the "proposition"—that "every
means effectual to preserve India from oppression is a guard
to preserve the British Constitution from its worst corruption"—and the "division" which isolates four main objections
to the Bill. These four topics then provide the core of Burke's
"confirmation": answers to the objections enable him to advance positive arguments in support of the Bill. The "peroration" is a panegyric on Fox himself.

This investigation is illuminating. It forces our attention
to the influence of classical tradition and training on an eighteenth-century orator; it underlines the care with which Burke
prepared his material and delivered it in a form he considered
appropriate; and it clarifies the logical structure of his argument. Indeed "logic" is the keynote of Professor Mahoney's
analysis: "the logical arrangement of ideas [in the narration]
is particularly notable"; the confirmation is "a masterpiece of
forceful argumentation and relentless logic"; the opposition's
objections are dealt with "in a logical order"; the necessary
conditions for removing the administration of India from the
East India Company are outlined "in an extremely logical
order"; and finally, before considering the peroration, Professor Mahoney states that Burke has addressed "his hearers on
an intellectual level throughout the speech." Only once does
he remark that Burke "constantly reinforces his logic with
emotional appeal"; he does not appraise that appeal, show
how it ratifies the logic, or consider the meaning of his
term "reinforce." In fact his analysis illustrates the dangers,

as well as the advantages, of relating the quality of a speech to a speaker's skill in employing "the classical ideal of form in oratory." The principal danger is that the contribution made by reason and intellect, judgment and logic, becomes all-important. It is manifestly of immense significance; it is not self-sufficient. The cursory mention of "emotional appeal" reminds us of the important and complementary factors which the formalist approach undervalues. Burke certainly wished to establish substantive ideas, but he also wished these to be memorable and to stir his listeners emotionally—he wished to address them as whole men, not merely as Houyhnhnms. Moreover he expresses a philosophy of life and of government in opposition to those of Fox's adversaries. Now, we must take not only the formal, but all these characteristics into account if we are to consider Burke's "style" in the comprehensive meaning given to that word by Raymond Williams; if indeed we are to argue that Burke's whole rhetorical manner is a warranty for the justice and genuineness of his appeal. Finally, since the speech was in response to a particular situation we must be alert to the nature of that situation in order to evaluate the subtle kind of relationship that existed when Burke spoke. We shall then be able to compare his speech with others in the debate and to advance the proper claims for his distinctive style.

Fox's speech (in *The Parliamentary History,* Vol. 23), when he sought leave to introduce his Bill on November 18, 1783, is one that really merits the description "logical." He marshals his evidence with care before building any argument on, or drawing any conclusions from it; he indulges occasionally in paradox or antithesis, but there are few other signs of linguistic distinction; he puts more emphasis on the economic aspects of the Company's affairs than on their effect on the lives of the Indian people; and though he denounces the "inhumanity, false policy, peculation and brutality" of the Indian administration, there is no evidence that these were more than concepts or that they were deeply felt. There is more balance, cogency of expression, and statement of general principle in the following sentence from Pitt's speech opposing the Bill, than in any from Fox's:

> Necessity was the plea for every infringement of human freedom; it was the argument of tyrants; it was the creed of slaves.

On the first reading two days later, Grenville forcefully urged the House to guard British liberty against the kind of infringement Fox was allegedly proposing: "Let them enter upon the consideration of its different clauses coolly, cautiously, and unwillingly, not with the precipitancy and ardour of plunderers, eager to grasp at, and to hold fast their prey." It is worth noting in passing that this peroration may have contributed something to the images of rapacity that occur in Burke's speech. Lord Apsley called attention to the Commons' responsibilities to the "natives" of India but, compared with Burke's later treatment of this subject, his concern lacked real feeling and was nearer to cliché. As the debate on the second reading proceeded, the response of speaker after speaker to the controversial situation became visible: Fox made an eloquent retort to Pitt's condemnation quoted above; references to rapacity multiplied; Pitt rated English liberty superior to the claims of distressed Indians; Sir Richard Hill, perhaps sensing the need for light relief, made a witty, though superficial, speech at Fox's expense; and Erskine brilliantly dealt with the charge that the Bill would infringe on the chartered rights of the Company.

These details make no pretense to be an adequate survey of the debate; they appear here only to support the observation that to estimate Burke's distinctive achievement his speech (on December 1) must be viewed in its original context. This done, one can begin to answer Williams' question, "why?" Why did Burke adopt a particular tone and mode of address? Why did he give special prominence to selected individuals or events? Why did he choose to reiterate certain key ideas or images? Answers to such questions allow us to assess his ability to respond to a specific situation, and his success in doing so.

It is not necessary to demonstrate exhaustively how Burke handles the main objections to Fox's Bill: that it was an attack on the Company's chartered rights, that it increased the power of the Crown or, alternatively, of the Ministry at the expense of the Crown, and that it deeply affected the national credit. Professor Mahoney has shown that he dealt with each clearly and logically. A complete examination of the speech would require us to compare Burke's handling of, say, the first objection with Erskine's, and to ask: does Burke contribute anything new or more compelling, more memorable or more permanently valuable? What can be attempted here, however, is a consideration of the nature of the experience provided by Burke's speech, the emphasis which distinguishes his from others, and the rhetorical methods he employs, for which "logical" is inadequate as a descriptive term.

Through the speech runs a theme which may be summarized in Burke's words: "thirty millions of my fellow-creatures and fellow-subjects." [4] The Indians are both "creatures" and "subjects"; they must be viewed as members of a political system and as human beings; they have privileges which relate to issues of power, charters, and national credit, but which also require the exercise of feeling, sensibility, sympathetic understanding, and imaginative participation in human distress. Thus for a critic to interest himself solely in matters relating to the Indians' status as "subjects" and its consequences for English politics is plainly inadequate. Burke's overriding interest in people who suffered or could benefit from British administration was a major and distinctive contribution to the debate. It produced a difference in tone—in sharp contrast both to Hill's witty effusions and the legalistic, unfeeling arguments of other opposition speakers—which was of notable significance. Moreover it would make a strong appeal to contemporaries inside and outside of Parliament who were sensitive to the plight of the oppressed. Cowper's letters, at least, support this conjecture. [5]

Associated with this humane solicitude for the Indian
people are two controlling but contrasting ideas: what might
be termed the civilized maturity of India and the barbarous
immaturity of the British rulers. Time and again Burke juxta-
poses these ideas. The Indian people are not

> an abject and barbarous populace . . . but a people for ages
> civilized and cultivated; cultivated by all the arts of polished
> life, whilst we were yet in the woods. There have been (and
> still the skeletons remain) princes once of great dignity, au-
> thority, and opulence. There are to be found the chiefs of
> tribes and nations. There is to be found an ancient and vener-
> able priesthood, the depository of their laws, learning and his-
> tory . . . a nobility of great antiquity and renown; a multitude
> of cities. . . .[6]

This passage, with its stress on culture, antiquity, and civilized achievement, describes the Indian people in general; the
same features reappear when Burke discusses individual men
or areas. The Great Mogul is

> amiable in his manners, respectable for his piety according to
> his mode, and accomplished in all the Oriental literature. . . .
> Money is coined in his name; in his name justice is adminis-
> tered; he is prayed for in every temple through the countries
> we possess.—But he was sold.[7]

Hafiz Rhamet—"as famous throughout the East for the ele-
gance of his literature, and the spirit of his poetical compositions . . . as for his courage"—was slaughtered; his head
was "delivered for money to a barbarian" and his family reduced to penury.[8] Benares, "the capital city of the Indian
religion" was "great in commerce and opulence"; it offered
an asylum for both "poverty and wealth" such "that the wisest laws and best assured free constitution could not better
provide."[9] This city was brutally seized. In the Carnatic the
Hindus carefully stored rain water in reservoirs from which
they irrigated their lands. With the coming of the East India

Company "hospitals fell to ruin; the reservoirs of water went to decay . . . and sterility, indigence, and depopulation, overspread the face of these once-flourishing provinces." [10]

Such passages are permeated by the ideas mentioned earlier. On the one hand there is the antiquity of the Indian civilization, its religious basis, its concern for peace, literature, and human well-being; on the other there is English rapacity and brutality, impiety and inhumanity, leading to sterility and ruin. The immaturity of British rule is stressed in Burke's contemptuous reference to "the boys we send to India." They are not worse "than the boys whom we are whipping at school, or that we see trailing a pike, or bending over a desk at home"; but "they drink the intoxicating draught of authority and dominion before their heads are able to bear it"; "they are full grown in fortune long before they are ripe in principle." [11] Later Burke expresses his horror at "the desperate boldness of a few obscure young men" who "tossed about, subverted, and tore to pieces, as if it were in the gambols of a boyish unluckiness and malice, the most established rights, and the most ancient and most revered institutions, of ages and nations." [12]

This contrast, often reiterated, is no mere debating trick; it is evidence of the civilized, mature humanity of the speaker himself. Where earlier speakers in the debate had referred to Indian distress, Burke is giving proof of personal involvement and genuine feeling; he felt these distresses on his pulses. As a consequence his language and the repetition of these central ideas provide a warranty of his honesty of purpose. Here is a further distinctive quality in his speech; one feels (unlike one's response to Grenville's utterance) that Burke was not playing factious politics, but that he meant profoundly and intensely what he said. What is thereby involved is "the credit of the relator," to use Burke's words of many years earlier,[13] and it is of major importance to the effectiveness of rhetorical discourse.

At certain significant moments there is a notable rise in intensity. For example, Burke contrasts the British with ear-

lier conquerors of India. The great difference he sees is that
the Asian invaders, unlike the British, gradually became identified with India and abated their ferocity; they could not en-
dure to live permanently among "poverty, sterility, and deso-
lation," or forever to suffer "the curses of a whole people";
and whatever pecuniary advantages were obtained remained
in India itself. "But under the English government all this
order is reversed. The Tartar invasion was mischievous; but it
is our protection that destroys India." [14] There is no end to
the crude greed of the English. Boys are sent out to govern;
they extort with boyish vigor; and every rupee they filch dis-
appears from India. Nothing is contributed to Indian life or
culture: "England has erected no churches, no hospitals, no
palaces, no schools; England has built no bridges, made no
high roads, cut no navigations, dug out no reservoirs." [15] As
this passionate onslaught continues Burke is eventually
compelled to articulate the revulsion he experiences at
having to make it: "it is an arduous thing to plead against
abuses of a power which originates from your own country,
and affects those whom we are used to consider as strangers."
Yet it is precisely this readiness to respond emotionally to
evidence of barbarity, as well as to use his intelligence, that
convinces one of his genuine purpose. A man holding Burke's
views *ought* to be disturbed: "I am sensible that a cold style
of describing actions which appear to me in a very affecting
light is equally contrary to the justice due to the people, and
to all genuine human feelings about them." [16]

This statement, in the assurance it gives to the audience
of the speaker's humanity and involvement, is comparable to
Swift's confession in *A Short View of the State of Ireland*—
"But my Heart is too heavy to continue this Irony longer" [17]
—where his detachment breaks down in the face of the mis-
ery of the Irish people. And we can be sure that Burke's dem-
onstration of emotion is not—to put it crudely—a gimmick.
His emotions are fully consonant with his theme which focuses on the humanity of the people for whom he pleads. His
own humane feelings give him the right to demand from the

Commons active consideration of the distress caused to thirty million people who are both creatures and subjects.

Burke recognizes, however, that it is difficult to enter sympathetically into the plight of people in a distant country: "Even the very names of the sufferers are so uncouth and strange to our ears." Consequently he gives prominence to selected people and places, using them in a quasi-symbolic manner to direct the thinking and feeling of his listeners. One is Warren Hastings, a man identified with Indian affairs but well known in England; two—the Carnatic and Bengal—are easily remembered names and provide vivid examples of English oppression; and finally, a group of women sufferers enables Burke again to test the humanity of his audience.

Hastings—to whom Professor Mahoney's critical procedure gives not a single mention—is Burke's central "character" in a full sense. Not only had he become notorious in Anglo-Indian affairs and in Parliamentary debates; not only was he the center of a deep cleavage of opinion and therefore provoked strong feelings; for Burke he also personified all the evils of the Company's rule in India. Hastings was not the name of a shadowy Indian potentate; it was a household term. By frequent reiteration it would become indelibly associated with oppression, inhumanity, and rapacity; indeed Burke intended that it should symbolize "one of the most corrupt and destructive tyrannies that probably ever existed in the world." [18] A House of Commons that rejected Fox's Bill would be implicated in that tyrannical corruption. The Carnatic—as is evident from previous references—is a symbolic instance of the aggressive self-interest of the Company. Burke sharply contrasts the glory, affluence, piety, and justice which formerly prevailed with the sterility produced by the Company's extortions and unfeeling exploitation. Similarly, Bengal is made prominent. In view of Burke's later concern with the merits of the *ancien régime* in France, it is interesting that he compares Bengal with that country, emphasizing the harmony that results from a traditional social hierarchy. The Indian province under the Company's rule thus comes to represent

the evils which follow from a wanton destruction of traditional order. In language strongly reminiscent of that used to
describe revolutionary France in the *Reflections,* Burke
speaks of the encouragement given to the greed of usurers,
jobbers, and schemers by the "state auctioneers" who sold
Bengal to the highest bidders. Finally, again recalling his
technique in the *Reflections,* Burke twice focuses his audience's attention on the plight of Indian women; their names
are less important than their symbolic defenselessness. Burke
could expect the principle of "the reverence paid to the fe-
male sex in general, and particularly to women of high rank
and condition" [19] to be acknowledged by his listeners; it had
been violated (an exact parallel with the case of Marie Antoi-
nette in 1789) by "a rapacious and licentious soldiery" acting on the Company's orders.

   At the center of these and other instances of tyranny is
Burke's denunciation of the Company's hypocrisy. Men like
Hastings and Benfield had been strongly condemned in public
by the Court of Directors but they had uniformly flourished;
on the other hand Burke remarks on the "state of insignifi-
cance and disgrace to which all of those have been reduced
whom [the Directors] approved." [20] What the people of India
fear most is English protection: British troops guard their
frontiers "not to exclude an enemy, but to prevent the escape
of the inhabitants." [21] Or, when the Company supports the
oppressive Nabob of Arcot, it entreats him to defend the
small traders whose protectors, the *polygars,* it had rooted
out. "When they extirpate the shepherd and the shepherd's
dog, they piously recommend the helpless flock to the mercy,
and even to the *tenderest care,* of the wolf." [22] The bitter
irony recalls other metaphors and images elsewhere in the
speech which carry ideas of remorseless cruelty and represent
the Company's agents as brutish adventurers acting by the
law of the jungle. But more immediately important, it underlines Burke's frequent use of paradox. One of his most urgent
arguments is that appearance and reality do not coincide: the
Company appears to give protection, in fact it is tyrannical;

men who seem to be condemned prosper, those apparently approved perish; what seems to be economic success proves to be bankruptcy, and so on. Nothing can be taken at face value; seeming and being are not identical. Paradox and irony are natural literary devices to use about such a situation. The literary method, in other words, is perfectly consonant with Burke's theme; indeed it is no mere stylistic ornament but stands in an organic relation to the theme itself.

"Hypocrisy is the only vice that cannot be cured." [23] This is the kernel of Burke's accusations. In stern contrast stands the speaker himself, claiming that his speech is "the pledge of [his] rectitude." [24] The Directors of the Company were unlikely even to "slip or deviate into rectitude" [25]—a bitter reminder of Dryden's *MacFlecknoe;* for his part, Burke's own honesty, disinterestedness, sense of justice, and benevolence are established by his literary manner. He pleads for justice and is obviously a just man; his rhetoric visibly guarantees it. His style, by its consistent clarity, logic, and evidence of natural, widely-shared emotions, is proof that he is no hypocrite. Seen from this point of view, his panegyric on Fox takes on a new significance. It is no mere eulogy of the mover of a Bill; it lays final emphasis on the very characteristic in Fox which, it is here claimed, Burke has established as his own by stylistic means. Fox has attempted "the rescue of the greatest number of the human race that were ever so grievously oppressed"; he has faults, but in them "there is no mixture of deceit, of hypocrisy, of pride . . . or want of feeling for the distresses of mankind," and he has "the enlargement to comprehend, the spirit to undertake, and the eloquence to support, so great a measure of hazardous benevolence." [26]

NOTES

1. Raymond Williams, *History and Theory*, IV (1965), pp. 380–381.
2. "It intends persons without virtue or sense, in all stations; and many of the highest rank are often meant by it" *(Tom Jones)*.
3. John L. Mahoney, "Edmund Burke and the East India Bill of Charles James Fox: The Classical Oration in the Service of Eighteenth-Century Politics," *The Burke Newsletter*, IV (Summer 1963), 210–219.
4. *The Works of the Right Honorable Edmund Burke*, IV (London: F. C. and J. Rivington, 1815), p. 114.
5. In a letter to William Unwin, January 3, 1784, Cowper remarks that the Company "make happiness of thirty millions of mankind, a consideration subordinate to that of their own emolument, oppressing them as often as it may serve a lucrative purpose, and in no instance . . . consulting their interest or advantage" (William Hayley, *Life and Letters of William Cowper*, II [Chichester: W. Mason, 1809], pp. 157–158). Also it is worth noting Professor Holden Furber's remark that Burke's letters of the 1780s "reinforce the view generally held in India today that Burke, not [Sir Philip] Francis, was the real champion of Bengal's downtrodden millions (Holden Furber, ed., *The Correspondence of Edmund Burke*, V [Cambridge: The University Press, 1965], p. xv). Nevertheless Burke viewed his task realistically: "If the whole Gentoo [Hindu] race had but one neck, [his countrymen] would see it cut with the most perfect indifference" *(Correspondence*, V, p. 151).
6. *Works, op. cit.*, p. 18.
7. *Ibid.*, p. 22.
8. *Ibid.*, p. 24.
9. *Ibid.*, p. 59.
10. *Ibid.*, pp. 78–80.
11. *Ibid.*, p. 41.
12. *Ibid.*, pp. 86–87.
13. H. V. F. Somerset, ed., *A Note-Book of Edmund Burke* (Cambridge: The University Press, 1957), p. 45.
14. *Works, op. cit.*, p. 39.
15. *Ibid.*, pp. 40–41.
16. *Ibid.*, p. 43. With reference to his panegyric on Burke himself in 1787, Sir Gilbert Elliot testifies to the effect on the Commons of the expression of strong and genuine emotion: "There was nothing either difficult or fine in the matter; but it may serve to prove what a powerful ingredient in eloquence a *sincere feeling*

in the speaker is" (The Countess of Minto, ed., *Life and Letters of Gilbert Elliot,* I [London: Longmans, Green, 1874], p. 177).

17. Herbert Davis, ed., *Irish Tracts* 1728–1733 (Oxford: Basil Blackwell, 1955), p. 10.
18. *Works, op. cit.,* p. 114.
19. *Ibid.,* p. 68.
20. *Ibid.,* p. 99.
21. *Ibid.,* p. 51.
22. *Ibid.,* p. 82.
23. *Ibid.,* p. 99.
24. *Ibid.,* p. 127.
25. *Ibid.,* p. 113.
26. *Ibid.,* pp. 128–129.

Of Style: Buffon
and Rhetorical Criticism

DONALD C. BRYANT

The nature of style as a quality pervading the whole of discourse and ultimately determining its meaning is the subject of this essay. The author grounds this concept in the writing of Count de Buffon, whose eloquent statement on style is rarely appreciated—style indeed is the man, but in a deeper and broader sense than the popular use of the phrase suggests.

Donald C. Bryant is Professor of Speech at the State University of Iowa. His article is revised from the original Western Speech *symposium.*

When the original of this essay appeared in *Western Speech* as part of the symposium on criticism, which forms the base of this volume, it seemed sensible to reassess style (elocution), the ancient third art or office of rhetoric, as a consideration in rhetorical criticism. Furthermore, at that time it seemed that reassessment must inevitably imply enhancement. Hardly could there have been occasion, it appeared, further to depress the repute of style in public address, or to relegate the selection and management of language to a more distant, peripheral province than it occupied in most professional rhetorical speculation, criticism, and pedagogical practice.

Ten years ago, even so, there were scattered signs of changing times. Cautiously, substantive instruction in style,

and sometimes even the term, had begun to reappear in textbooks for college and university students of public speaking.
In the first edition of a popular textbook, for example, the
precepts for the management of the staples of discourse—
words, sentences, and paragraphs; figures, images and
rhythms—had been cautiously insinuated into such functional categories as "interest," "attention," and "suggestion."
In a second, revised edition, these materials were disengaged
and reassembled with additions in a separate chapter, not entitled "Style," to be sure, but "Language," though the word
style appears undisguised in the first paragraph. In a later edition still, the chapter is actually entitled "Style." Small matters, of course, and not very important! But there was encouragement to be found in the pedagogy of public speaking,
and perhaps in the practice of public address, as the sense
seemed to reemerge that cultivation of efficiency and grace in
language was not necessarily deprecation of thought, of substance; that attention to the selection and management of
words did not inevitably imply indifference to the quality (or
the existence) of things.

In mature rhetorical criticism also, style, as a matter of
serious consideration, had reappeared unobtrusively in a firm,
incisive section of Marie Hochmuth [Nichols]'s introductory
essay to the third volume of the *History and Criticism of
American Public Address* (1955). Though the section came
in the latter part of the essay and comprised less than a sixth
of the whole, it clearly established the principle that the
choices, the options, in language which the rhetorical discourse exhibits determine its final meaning.

Professor Nichols' position was clear and unqualified,
though developed in moderate proportions—a happily reas-
serted commonplace, or so it should have seemed. The essay-
ists who followed her in the volume, however, and most of
those who had contributed to the preceding two volumes,
though they differed widely in their treatment of the speech as
finally composed, seemed in varying degrees and in varying
ways unhappy with the problem of style. They approached

style with gingerly criteria; they saluted it in passing with orthodox, even deferential vocabulary; they labeled certain of
its traditional constituents and illustrated them accurately;
they offered passages for admiration or amusement; but almost always they backed away from what would seem to be
the central critical questions, or struck them but glancing
blows in the twilight. What are the elements in discourse
which may usefully be considered the constituents of style, as
distinct from those other factors which rhetorical critics commonly analyze or indentify under the rubric of invention, disposition, delivery, and such? How does style interact with the
other factors to create the full force and meaning of the discourse? What do (or may) the selection and management of
language in fact accomplish towards the quality of the speech
and towards tapping the potential sources of response which
may be presumed available in the potential audience?

I make these observations in no mood of derogation or
reproach. Those essays represented and still represent the
most substantial recent efforts in the rhetorical criticism of
oratory. Together they bespeak an admirable decade of development in both principle and execution. Only with humility as clear-minded as possible is it worth while at any time to
confront the most difficult problems of criticism. One of these
is the problem of knowing enough—history, sociology, eco-
nomics, literature, psychology, rhetoric—to recreate the max-
imum relevant context of public address. The critics are mas-
tering this problem, perhaps erratically and slowly, but
nevertheless—though not without occasional fanatic resort
to simplistic formulas. The other great problem, the one
which I am attempting to approach on a spiral course, is
also a problem of knowing. More especially, however, it demands the capacity to breed insights where much of the evidence dies as it is born and most of it fades or changes under
examination—the problem of style. Hence, in the end the
critic's art is only less strenuous and hazardous than the one
he treats, and his ineptitudes and failures only less frequent—

and honorable—than the writer's and orator's. Perhaps it would be unjust to observe, after Dryden, that critics are generated from the corruption of orators. Nevertheless, the evidence in print ten years ago, and now, requires us to admit that it is easy to theorize and hard to criticize; easy to adumbrate a "new approach" to rhetorical criticism, and difficult to get there; far safer to enunciate objectives and principles than to analyze discourse—especially style.

The past decade seems gently to have accelerated the reinfusion of style into rhetorical speculations. It may be that the meteoric passage of John F. Kennedy has had some effect on potential response to the language of public address. Perhaps in his inaugural address, for example, and in other presidential speeches, he confirmed in audiences, and in some rhetorical critics, what Adlai Stevenson had only begun to reteach them—that the quality of language is the substance of a speaker's message. Contemporaneously, rhetorical criticism, both theoretical and practical, is taking modest steps toward a more sophisticated treatment of style. Professor Nichols, in her *Rhetoric and Criticism* (1963), reenforces her earlier position. Edwin Black, in *Rhetorical Criticism* (1965), sees the essence of certain kinds of rhetorical discourse as accessible only through analysis of the texture of the language, the style. Finally, James T. Boulton, though not professing rhetorical criticism, exemplifies the relevance of style to the primary achievements of political discourse in *The Language of Politics in the Age of Wilkes and Burke* (1963).

The foregoing are good signs. The unfortunate scarcity, however, of rhetorical criticism of serious proportions, and especially of stylistic criticism, still appears to justify sober reassessment and, what in essence may amount to the same thing, redefinition. The phenomena of discourse tend to remain constant as the terms for studying them or avoiding or overlooking them shift and change, even as the term *rhetoric* itself, and the critics of a specific place and time become securely stockaded within their own categories. Whatever the

categories, however, the critic always finds himself somehow
trying to analyze the mystery by which the constituents of
communication finally grow into living discourse. He knows,
or senses, that the rhetorical artifact, like the poetic artifact,
is characteristically a creation in language and that somewhere in or around the language lies the animate principle of
the discourse, pervading all the other principles. Thus the theorist or critic who sets out methodically to use the categories
of Cicero or Aristotle or the strategies or pentad of Kenneth
Burke finds himself discussing the elements of *elocutio,*
whether his specific focus at any given moment be on invention, disposition, memory, or delivery; on pathetic proofs,
ethical proofs, or logical proofs; on strategies of confidence,
indignation, or extenuation. That is, style, like diction in the
Aristotelian constituents of drama, pervades all. Conversely,
the critic who takes only style for his subject begins almost at
once to invade the provinces of the other categories such as
thought and organization, whether confessedly like Buffon, or
against his own specific denial, like Somerset Maugham on
Edmund Burke.[1]

Is this merely to reassert the axiom that the whole is
greater than the sum of the parts; that discourse is organic,
and that a speech is like a living creature with a body, head,
and feet, with a single principle of vitality through the whole
body; that in all artificial systems the categories must inevitably commit upon each other the offenses of invasion and ex-
clusion? Perhaps in part, but not merely. The evidence provided by the history of rhetoric, by the explicit testimony of
such men as Cicero, Isocrates, and the majority of their successors, and the practice of critics of oratory until the last
generation enforce the conclusion that in the criticism of the
verbal art of discourse, style, though not the primary category, may very well be the ultimate category.

I do not propose to offer a new system of methodology
for the criticism of style; space would be too short even if
need suggested it. No more will I reassemble a check list of

the devices and forms of language which the critic may expect to find at work in the discourse he has under consideration. Of course, the inherited tools and procedures of critical analysis should always be improved on, but they are abundant, from Aristotle and the *Ad Herennium* to the latest "rhetoric" or introduction to poetry. They may be used well or ill, with subtlety and sophistication or with mechanical sterility. They are still but tools, however, the keys for entries into the discourse, through which the critic may gain access to the functional phenomena which are style.

New help is ever forthcoming. Semantics, information theory, the formulas of propaganda analysis, studies and experiments in the psychology of language, and communication research are all seeking new tools for the observation of language in action, or are busy redesigning and renaming familiar shopworn tools (which may amount to much the same thing). They are teaching the rhetorical critic, if he will but submit to learning, not only how to "name his tools," but how to use them. From the work of the linguistic philosophers, the behavioral scientists, and the New Critics especially, the rhetorical critic may not only modernize his equipment, but even clarify his objectives, so long as he keeps himself clear of the limitation of specialized cultism.[2]

The instrumental techniques and materials for the criticism of style, to be sure, must be mastered. Even the routine application of them leads along the way toward the subtlety we pursue, for one must begin somewhere. The result which we want, however, will be dependent upon a conception of style as the factor in discourse which makes it discourse, which gives actuality to the logic and dialectic, the pathos and ethos; which gives life to the potentiality of things and of thought.

That kind of conception might be revived from a new look at almost any of the traditional theorists and teachers whose names support the consequence of rhetorical scholarship. I choose, however, one who enters too seldom into rhe-

torical discussions, the eighteenth-century French naturalist
Buffon in his address to the French Academy (1753).

Buffon's most famous dictum, the only one, in fact, which
can be said to have any general currency, is the well-known
aphorism, "The style is the man himself." [3] Usually quoted
out of context, it may be interpreted, of course, as confirming
that familiar divorce between matter and manner, between
thought and language, between the man and his message,
which supports deprecation of skill with words: "Adlai Stevenson was a fine man, of course, but what had he to offer but
style?" Even from a consideration of the aphorism out of
context, however, a crucial idea about the functions of style
may be suggested. If the ethos of a speaker or writer, the
apparent character which he exhibits in his discourse, is his
strongest source of conviction in his audience, and if the style
is the man himself, then style is seen to be the primary vehicle
of the ethical mode of proof.

Neither interpretation correctly represents Buffon's intention, which was to assign a more comprehensive mission to
style, no less than the *creation* of permanent truths. In context the sentence appears thus:

> The well-written works are the only ones that will go down
> to posterity: the amount of knowledge in a book, the peculiar-
> ity of the facts, the novelty even of the discoveries are not
> sure warrants of immortality, . . . since the knowledge, facts,
> and discoveries, being easily detached, are passed on to others,
> and even gain intrinsically when appropriated by more gifted
> hands. These things are external to the man; the style is the
> man himself. Style, then, can be neither detached, nor trans-
> ferred nor altered by time. . . . It is truth alone that is per-
> manent. Now a beautiful style is such in fact only by the in-
> finite number of truths that it presents. All the intellectual
> graces residing in it, all the interdependences of which it is
> composed, are truths not less useful, and for the human spirit
> possibly more precious, than those, whatsoever they be, that
> form the core of the subject.

Buffon, of course, is discussing good style, even great style; and style may be, and too frequently is, indifferent or bad. Its relation to the worth and meaning of the speech, however, is still the same. What the speaker says achieves its final meaning from the way he says it. The ridiculous false-hood of much radio and television advertising lies as much in the style as in the intention. The truth that soap is useful for washing cannot sustain the extravagance of verbiage heaped upon it without becoming a substantive lie. On the other hand, the equally common truths of national loyalty and fu-neral sobriety, recreated and transformed by Lincoln's style, become monumental ideals for generations. How these changes happen through the medium of language and which qualities of the style are the transforming agents are ultimate problems of the rhetorical criticism of discourse.

Buffon's characterization of style as the man himself ap-pears toward the end of his discourse. It is preceded by other more significant and comprehensive ideas. His first definition of style, for example, is so brief and plain that one may over-look its critical implications: "Style is simply the order and movement one gives to one's thoughts." Perhaps this is the achievement of the whole of rhetoric, the whole art of verbal communication. But let us recall that Buffon was not thinking of style as a category in rhetorical theory. He was discussing style as a factor in a composition, in a discourse. "Order and movement"—taken together these are dynamic terms, terms of life and action controlled by form, and the "discourse-ishness" of discourse *is* its order and movement through lan-guage towards an intended end with an intended audience. Further implications of Buffon's definition may be pursued, but its emphasis upon style as the vital, the incarnating factor cannot be far from right. The rhetorical critic must describe and appraise this factor if he is to proceed beyond a learned exhibition of classified ingredients to an estimate of the whole live discourse.

In the technical vocabulary of rhetoric, one may object,

perhaps, that to adopt Buffon's scope is to make *dispositio* part of *elocutio,* or simply a phase of it, and even to permit *elocutio* to poach upon *inventio.* Again one must admit that the objection has force, especially if one is reluctant to tamper with the Ciceronian categories. Here, however, the purposes of the rhetorical theorist must be distinguished from those of user of rhetorical theory, the critic. It is difficult at best to consider the functioning language of discourse without becoming involved immediately with the ordering of the discourse. Furthermore, if we go beyond the static idea of disposition as arrangement to the potentially dynamic idea of disposition as *disposing,* as Russell Wagner thought necessary, we may conclude that for the critic the two names signify the two amplifiers for a stereophonic study of a single factor in discourse. This factor is best conceived as style because that name suggests the foundation of discourse in language. "Disposition," said Wagner, *"is* concerned with the principles of disposing (in the sense of using) the materials invented for a speech, in the best possible manner, for the purpose of effecting the end intended by the speaker in any given situation." In Cicero's idea of disposition, one of the three distinguishable purposes is the "massing and shaping, expanding, contracting, proportioning, and emphasizing, coloring and toning, according to the special circumstances of the speech." [4] Without the label of *dispositio* upon such statements it would be hard to suppose that we were not speaking of style. "Style in painting," wrote Sir Joshua Reynolds in his second discourse before the Royal Academy, "is the same as in writing, a power over materials, whether words or colors, by which conception or sentiments are conveyed." I do not know that Reynolds was acquainted with Buffon's discourse or had it at his elbow when he composed his second discourse, but it is easy to read Reynolds' statement as a paraphrase of Buffon's "order and movement which we give to our ideas."

　　One cause for the slighting of style among rhetorical critics, or more often the depressing of it and the excessive narrowing of its scope, has been the sort of protective tariff erected to secure their infant industry against foreign imports from literary criticism. This estimable precaution, the origin of which, perhaps, lay partly in a misinterpretation of certain ideas in Wichelns' classic essay, hardly needs preserving and should now be taken no more seriously than the figure in the preceding sentence suggests. Another more important cause is one which the passage of time alone will not remove: the strong popular suspicion, to some extent shared by rhetorical critics themselves, that style is at best decoration and at worst an unintellectual black magic through which nothing is made to appear something, and malice, stupidity, and falsehood take on the countenance of virtue. Of course, if style is the man himself and if men are scalawags and demagogues, style is liable to the charge. The morality of a speaker is most plainly evident in his style. One may smile and smile and seem a villain still.

Buffon, again, may help the rhetorical critic regain his perspective. The critic need not obscure the functional significance of stylistic considerations by forcing them into the more respectable intellectual category of invention or by approaching them primarily as data in the analysis of the Aristotelian modes of proof. "To write well—it is at once to think deeply," says Buffon, "to feel vividly, and to express clearly; it is to have at once intelligence, sensibility, and taste. Style supposes the united exercise of all the intellectual faculties." If those intellectual faculties are feeble or misshapen, the style cannot but be so too, and it will exhibit those qualities to the critic.

Of course, the critic must learn to cope with certain popular conceptions of style which have tended to limit the resources of analysis. One of the milder and more innocuous of these has had a long history in both literary and rhetorical theory: the idea that style is the decoration or sweetening of thought. In this view, attractive especially because it is easy to explain, style is conceived as paint upon the materials of thought or feeling, as cement into which the parts of the mosaic may be set, as flavor somehow diffused through the products of invention without really entering into them. A better figure might suppose a transforming chemical which creates essential properties: color, constituency, texture, giving identity to the whole.

Here it may be useful to distinguish *style* as I am using the term from two more of the popular competitive meanings —eccentricity and fashion. Neither is style in the broad sense, but each may contribute the most readily identifiable elements in the linguistic behavior of any given speaker, writer, or era. Individual eccentricity showed, for example, in the repetitive, overlapping phrases, clauses, and sentences in the oral performance of the late Joseph R. McCarthy; and English writers and speakers in the eighteenth century tended to exhibit those triplets and balances which make most British speakers and writers of the time hardly distinguishable by the novice.

But let us return to the heart of the matter. Style makes discourse out of the materials of invention; the facts of the case become the facts of discourse when transformed by style. This transformation, or actually creation, is well illustrated in the manuscripts of Edmund Burke. There revision after revision, emendation of emendation, casting out and rewriting, correction upon change appear until one needs a magnifying glass to search for the final text—the final *written* text only, for the speeches as delivered represented further refinements, growth, and adaptation still. Most of the changes were not what would be generally called substantive, but like the revisions of the poet, they evince Burke's struggle for the ultimate "right" meaning, which he felt but probably did not fully apprehend until, in Swift's words, it was born with "proper words in proper places." The materials of invention, imitation, or merely collection, be the composer's method what they may, are recreated, for better or for worse, in the act of composition. Robert Oppenheimer, in a passage quoted by Professor Nichols, wrote:

It is style which complements affirmation with limitation and humility; it is style which makes it possible to act effectively, but not absolutely; it is style which . . . enables us to find a harmony between the pursuit of ends essential to us, and a regard for the views, the sensibilities, the aspirations of those to whom the problem may appear in another light; it is above all style through which power defers to reason.[5]

When the critic is coming to grips with his subject, no Buffon or Nichols, no Oppenheimer or Reynolds can prescribe for him the emphasis and proportions which the several critical categories ought to assume in his analysis. With the aid of such resources as he can muster, he must strive to see the discourse for what it was and what it is. He will listen to the voices of the theorists, but he will look at the phenomena through his own eyes and listen to the silent sounds of discourse with his own inner ear. If he listens to the voice of this essay, perhaps he will make a free rather than rigid use of "all the available means of" judgment; perhaps he will separate matter from manner, thought from style and delivery, *inventio* from *dispositio* and *elocutio,* only so far as the separate treatment helps him keep his mind in order and not so far as to keep it in leading strings. If the voice seems to shout too loudly the word *style,* let him remember that in this essay it is style that we are considering and not all of rhetoric or all of discourse. Furthermore, there is much in contemporary rhetorical criticism to suggest that overstatement on this topic may be mildly salutary, rather than harmful.

We have been accustomed to praise the rhetoric of St. Augustine, for example, or of Thomas Wilson or James A. Winans for its reassertion of the primacy of invention. That praise is just; but the same sort of praise would be just were we considering the theory of poetry, painting, architecture, sculpture, or any of the arts. Where the substance is not good, it cannot sustain the creation. But perhaps the critic will come closest to grappling with the distinctiveness of the rhetorical work if he considers more attentively than has been his wont the idea of style as the order and movement which we give to our thoughts. Style must not, it cannot usurp the principal place in the attention of the rhetorical critic, but it deserves a place only less than coordinate with invention, of which it accomplishes the ultimate fruition. Style is the final elaboration of meaning.[6]

NOTES

1. Somerset Maugham, "After Reading Burke," in *The Vagrant Mood: Six Essays* (Garden City, New York: Doubleday, 1953), pp. 133–166.
2. If one *were* recommending models for the analysis and criticism of prose style, rhetorical or not, one would refer often to the principles and practice of William Wimsatt, Jr., in his *Prose Style of Samuel Johnson* (New Haven: Yale University Press, 1941) and to James Sutherland's *On English Prose* (Toronto: University of Toronto Press, 1957).
3. For this and the subsequent quotations from Buffon, I use Lane Cooper's translation in his *Theories of Style* (New York: Macmillan, 1907), pp. 170–178.
4. Russell H. Wagner, "The Meaning of Dispositio," in *Studies in Speech and Drama in Honor of Alexander M. Drummond* (Ithica: Cornell University Press, 1944), pp. 293, 289.
5. Robert Oppenheimer, "The Open Mind," *The Bulletin of Atomic Scientists,* V (January 1949), 5.
6. W. K. Wimsatt, Jr., *The Prose Style of Samuel Johnson* (New Haven: Yale University Press, 1941), pp. 11, 63. In oral discourse, delivery, though ordinarily considered separately, as in pedagogy, obviously functions as an essential aspect of style.

Literary and
Rhetorical Criticism

ROBERT D. CLARK

Literary criticism has produced an immense and respectable literature, representing a variety of theories and methods. Despite obvious differences between rhetorical and literary discourse, certain principles apply—with different emphases—to both. Robert Clark brings to bear on rhetorical criticism the thinking of certain literary critics on form, the psychology of the audience, and the making of value judgments—enduring problems in the creation and evaluation of discourse.

Robert D. Clark is Professor of Speech and President of San Jose State College. His article is reprinted from the original Western Speech *symposium, where it appeared under the title "Lessons from the Literary Critics."*

In the early 1920s students of rhetoric declared their independence of literary and historical criticism. In an address before the National Association of Teachers of Speech, Professor Hoyt Hudson insisted that the orator must be measured by his effect on the audience.[1] A year or so later Herbert Wichelns in a scholarly essay on the "Literary Criticism of Oratory" rejected the three common approaches to the criticism of oratory: the biographical, which utilized the orations in the study of the mind and personality of the man; the historical, which drew upon the orations to illuminate the times; and the literary, which was concerned with the stylistic qualities of the oration and the question, "Is this oration literature?" "Oratory," Wichelns said, in concert with Hudson, "is not concerned with permanence, nor yet with beauty. It is concerned with effect." [2]

The literary critic's neglect of oratory and the historian's lack of interest in the oration as an art form have encouraged the student of rhetoric to develop his own critical discipline. In the long run, this consequence will be good, but the more immediate result has been the production of a criticism which adheres too closely to the formal *topoi;* it is frequently stereotyped, occasionally banal. In recent years an increasing number of students of public address have turned to literary critics for new insights and for a better understanding of their own art. Literary criticism has come a long way since Wichelns published his essay. Without attempting to limit our remarks to any special canon of "New Critics" or to be governed simply by developments since 1920, we wish to consider some of the lessons we can learn from the literary critics.

First, we can learn that form transcends the rhetorical categories. We recently had the unhappy experience of reading a diagnostic paper, a "case study" of a campaign oration given early in the career of an American orator. The writer ingeniously confessed that the speech was without significance, save as it was related to the career of the speaker. He then straightway abandoned the essential point, the one least doubtful justification on which he might have hung his analysis—the effect of the speech on the speaker—and proceeded to a commentary based on the Aristotelian *topoi.* One shudders to think how many such case studies might be spawned. Ought not critics, rather than use speeches to illustrate Aristotle, use Aristotle to understand and illuminate speeches and speakers?

There is a dynamic quality to form, a psychological function, that cannot be apprehended in the recognition and labeling of the several parts. Nor is it sufficient to append a discussion of the effect of the oration, if effect, as is so frequently the case, is judged upon historical evidence rather than upon analysis of the relation of the formal content to the effect. Kenneth Burke has attracted the attention of a growing number of students of rhetoric, not, one suspects, because of his insistence that literature is rhetorical rather than "pure," nor because he has grounded his *Rhetoric of Motives* in classical rhetoric, but because of his emphasis upon the relation of language to the psychology of the audience. Some years ago, in *Counter-Statement* he expressed his basic idea in simplified form.[3] Using the first act of *Hamlet* as an illustration, he showed how the audience, apprised of the situation, waited consciously or unconsciously for the Ghost to appear. In the fourth scene the moment has been definitely promised. Hamlet's friends have established the hour as twelve. There are sounds off-stage; of course it is not the ghost, but the sound of the king's carousal, for the king "keeps wassail." "A tricky and useful detail," says Burke. "We have been waiting for a ghost, and yet, startlingly, a blare of trumpets. And, once the trumpets are silent, we feel how desolate are these three men waiting for a ghost, on a bare 'platform,' feel it by this sudden juxtaposition of an imagined scene of lights and merriment."

Hamlet and Horatio converse. And suddenly Horatio exclaims: "Look, my Lord, it comes," "All this time," says Burke, "we had been waiting for a ghost, and it comes at the moment which was not pointing towards it. This ghost, so assiduously prepared for, is yet a surprise. And now that the ghost has come, we are waiting for something further."

Commenting on the illustration, Burke says: ". . . the psychology here is not the psychology of the *hero,* but the psychology of the *audience.* And by that distinction, form would be the psychology of the audience. Or, seen from another angle, form is the creation of an appetite in the mind of the auditor, and the adequate satisfying of that appetite. . . ." And later: "The method most natural to the psychology of form is eloquence." Content, organization, style are to be judged, not of themselves, but within this frame of reference.

Let us illustrate by reference to ethos in persuasion. The critic has not dispatched his responsibility when he has identified the ethical appeals, nor yet when he has said that through ethos the speaker has fulfilled at least one of the functions of the introduction—that of winning a favorable hearing. John Crowe Ransom has a useful distinction between syntax and "dystax." [4] Syntax is the logical progression of ideas; dystax is the digressive and antithetical emotion or mood, which seems to work at cross purposes to hinder or prevent the essential progression, but which in the end is seen not to thwart but to emphasize and heighten, perhaps ennoble the idea. Ethos is a kind of dystax. It gets in the way of the logical progression of the argument, is a constant source of irritation to the reader removed a hundred years from the charged atmosphere of the courtroom or the hysterical fervor of a nominating convention. In the cool retrospect of time the thrust and counter-thrust too often seem mere pretense, the showmanship of verbal dexterity. Take for example, one of the least offensive: Webster's magnificent reply to Hayne.[5] Webster smarted for two days while the impetuous and arrogant Hayne derided him for his mistaken analogy to Nathan Dane and taunted him with citation after citation of New England's defection in 1812. He had reason enough to understand the gravity of the situation and the seriousness of the challenge to himself. In consequence, for the first several minutes of his reply he was concerned with ethos.

Webster's most effective thrust, no doubt, was in response to Hayne's reference to Banquo's ghost. Hayne got off the allusion in a single sentence: "Has the ghost of the murdered Coalition come back, like the ghost of Banquo, to 'sear the eyeballs' of the gentleman, and will it not 'down at his bidding?' " Webster took a thousand words to reply. He knew how telling that allusion was, how tenacious the people's belief in the collusion between Adams and Clay. And how cleverly he turned Shakespeare to his own use, not simply to refute, but to help rebuild his own prestige.

Now all of this had nothing to do with the argument, not

even upon the grounds which Webster chose to debate, but in that period of the "grand oratory" it had much to do with Webster's status with his public. And as Aristotle well knew, no platform member gets a hearing for his logic unless he first commands a respect for his sagacity. It is vain to write this off as exhibitionism or to explain it, as the sociologists do, as simply striving for status. It is equally vain to discuss it as a sub-division of the introduction to the speech. In its formal aspect it is significant only as form is dynamic, as it relates to the psychology of the audience.

Second, we can learn that insight and understanding come only from a close reading of the text. If the New Critics have made a significant contribution to criticism, as I believe they have, it is chiefly through a close reading of the text, through a technique borrowed, with refinements, from the French, *explication de texte*. For illustration one might turn with equal profit to any of a number of recent critics, but consider for a moment William Empson's now familiar reading of a single line from Shakespeare, the last of the following verse:

> That time of year thou may'st in me behold
> When yellow leaves, or none, or few, do hang
> Upon those boughs which shake against the cold,
> Bare ruin'd choirs, where late the sweet birds sang.

Mr. Empson says: "Because ruined monastery choirs are places in which to sing, because they involve sitting in a row, because they are made of wood, are carved into knots and so forth, because they used to be surrounded by a sheltering building crystallized out of the likeness of a forest . . ." [6] this line has beauty. And so he continues, reading a richness of meaning into the line that would escape most of us.

One does not easily plumb the depth of good poetry, or of good metaphor in poetry, even with many readings. In oratory, although the figure must not be trite, it must, if it is to embody eloquence, be simple enough to be instantly perceived. One would prefer Herbert Spencer's concept of "economy" of style to Mr. Ransom's figure of cross traffic. [7]

The metaphor, instead of delaying the thought, advances it at a considerably accelerated pace. A whole welter of associated ideas and feelings may be compressed, may be "crystallized" as J. Middleton Murry puts it, into the single metaphor.[8] The resultant communication is not only quickened, but heightened emotionally. In oratory, not only must this matter of instant perception be considered, but the whole context in which the metaphor rests—not just the logical sequence—but the audience situation; its drama and spectacle, the tension of emotion and conflict. Take for example Bryan's speech at the Democratic Nominating Convention of 1896, no consequential argument, but a cliché-ridden refutation spoken as only Bryan could speak, capped with the most famous metaphor in American oratory: "You shall not press down upon the brow of labor this crown of thorns, you shall not crucify mankind upon a cross of gold." If this figure produced more of convention frenzy than of the ecstacy of which Longinus wrote—and it is not so different from the example Longinus cites from Hyperides—it certainly possessed that quality of an electric shock which so delighted audiences and critics of oratory of the last century. Less spectacular but probably more effective is the figure which Lincoln, borrowing from Jesus, used to open his campaign of 1858: "A house divided against itself cannot stand." It was a figure, not only instantly meaningful to the audience, but, as Roy Basler says, one "which carried in careful phrases an unforgettable image with implications of something more than rational analysis could maintain." [9] Mr. Basler traces its effect upon the campaign, and the sputtering and sarcastic attempts of Douglas to answer it—a study which is suggestive, but which needs further exploration.

These examples, although in some degree instantly perceptible, are subject to intensive reading. And one should not forget that the simple parables of Jesus, spoken by a carpenter in his efforts to communicate to a peasant audience, have prompted thousands of interpretations of their meanings. It is not enough for the rhetorical critic to identify these figures or to tabulate kinds or to list the subject matter sources, he must read intensively (not *in toto,* of course, but selectively) for the communication, for the effect upon the audience.

Third, we must face the question, ought we to assume the responsibility of making value judgments? The literary critics are somewhat less than in accord on this question. The Chicago school may insist that the poem be judged by its formal intrinsic qualities, rather than by its adherence to any general philosophical position. I. A. Richards, at least in his early period, and the psychological critics may, like the rhetoricians, judge a piece of literature for its effect. The New Critics, a category hard to accept definitively, are said to be Platonists.[10] Attentive as they are to the close reading, the texture of the poem, they are no less concerned with the question of ultimacy. Yvor Winters lays down the dictum that "The poet . . . must make a rational statement about an experience, and as rationality is a part of the medium, the ultimate value of the poem will depend in a fair measure on the soundness of the rationality. . . ."[11] On that basis he pronounces Robert Frost, a "Spiritual Drifter," one who "believes that impulse is trustworthy and reason contemptible, that formative decisions should be made casually and passively, . . . that ideas of good and evil need not be taken very seriously." The result, in his didactic poems, is "perversity and incoherence of thought," in his narratives, either a "slightness" or "a flat and uninteresting apprehension of the subject," and in his symbolic lyrics "a disturbing dislocation between the descriptive surface, which is frequently lovely, and the ultimate meaning, which is usually sentimental and unacceptable."[12]

Whatever we may think of such pronouncements in poetics, we may more properly expect them in rhetoric. For oratory, at least deliberative or forensic oratory, is scarcely an art in the sense that a poem is. It is a more practical art, if not the art of cookery or flattery, at least it is an instrument for social control. As such, it might well be tested both for its methods and its ends. And so, brilliant young historians like Richard Current or Richard Hofstadter deal harshly with John

Calhoun, the "Marx of the Master Class," the oratorical metaphysician whose ideas were inimical to a democratic society.[13] And Robert Merton, a sociologist, not only analyzes the techniques by which Kate Smith wheedled 60 million dollars out of her public in the third War Bond Drive, but he goes on to charge his professional colleagues, the social-psychologists, with the responsibility of making value-judgments, of asking themselves: are not the techniques which you taught Kate Smith destructive of the very society in which they operate? [14]

As speech critics we have been more timid. Oratory, we say, is to persuade. Ought it not be judged, then, in terms of its persuasiveness? Or, others ask, should it not be analyzed and judged as an art form on the principles prescribed by its discipline? Both questions are really an evasion. Effectiveness is more than tears and laughter. The discipline of rhetoric, Aristotle said, is derived from two other disciplines; dialectic and ethics. He cribbed a bit from his own works, from the *Analytics* and the *Nichomachean Ethics,* to find the syllogism of probabilities and ethical propositions, the raw stuff from which oratory must be made. He saw rhetoric as self corrective; given a rhetoric as skillful as that accorded evil, truth would prevail. The skillful orator would expose the false premises and logical fallacies of his opponent. The antagonist, then, is critic—and in the retrospect of history, the critic must sometimes be antagonist and protagonist. I do not see how the rhetorical critic, within the frame of his own discipline, can escape this responsibility. This does not mean either that he must judge orators of the past on the premises approved by his own generation nor that he should ignore the present in assessing the past.

In conclusion, we should like to add two admonitions. First, criticism is an art, not the raw tables or summaries of scholarship. The scholarship is a necessary prerequisite, and the formal reports, the compilations of the learned monograph, are essential to criticism. We have too much of unimaginative word counting, the pedestrian assemblage of argu-

ments, the methodical and generalized commentary laid out
on the Aristotelian pattern. Much of the New Criticism is ex-
citing reading, and as such it serves an important recreative
function of bringing literature to life. Now and then, as in
Brigance's *Jeremiah Black,* we achieve the same end.[15] But
we need more of good writing.

Second, we ought not conceive of rhetorical criticism too
formally. Wayne Shumaker summarizes the comparable problem of the literary critics in a single question: is literary criticism, as was once pretty generally accepted, to "measure literary works against accepted canons of aesthetic, rhetorical,
and moral propriety," or is it "any intelligent discussion of
literature?"[16] Rhetorical criticism may include a discussion
of the effect of the oration as a whole, or it may be an ap-
prisal on canons inductively perceived, but it is both more
and less—it is an intelligent discussion of oratory in the situation, oratory as spectacle, or of any one or more of the variety of *topoi* available to the critic.

NOTES

1. Hoyt Hudson, "Rhetoric and Poetry," *Quarterly Journal of Speech Education*, X (April 1924), 143–154; see also, "The Field of Rhetoric," *Quarterly Journal of Speech Education*, IX (April 1923), 167–180.
2. Herbert Wichelns, "The Literary Criticism of Oratory," in *Studies in Rhetoric and Public Speaking in Honor of James Albert Winans*, A. M. Drummond, ed. (New York: Century, 1925), pp. 181–216.
3. Kenneth Burke, "Psychology and Form," in *Counter-Statement* (Chicago: University of Chicago Press, 1953), pp. 29–31.
4. John Crowe Ransom, *The New Criticism* (Norfolk, Connecticut: New Directions, 1941), pp. 69–74.
5. Daniel Webster, "Second Speech on Foote's Resolution," in *The Works of Daniel Webster*, III (Boston: Little, Brown, 1866), 271–277.
6. William Empson, *Seven Types of Ambiguity* (London: Chatto and Windus, 1930), p. 3. The Chicago Critics justifiably protest that the psychological critics give undue attention to the detail and so neglect the form. See Elder Olson, "William Empson, Contemporary Criticism and Poetic Diction," in *Critics and Criticisms Ancient and Modern*, R. S. Crane, ed. (Chicago: University of Chicago Press, 1952), pp. 45–82.
7. Herbert Spencer, *The Philosophy of Style* (Boston, New York, and Chicago: Allyn and Bacon, 1917), pp. 1–4, 21–28. Ransom's treatment of Richards' concepts *tenor* and *vehicle* is over-simplified. See I. A. Richards, *The Philosophy of Rhetoric* (New York: Oxford University Press, 1936), pp. 96–138.
8. J. Middleton Murry, *The Problem of Style* (London: H. Milford, 1930), pp. 71–194.
9. Roy Basler, ed., *Abraham Lincoln: His Speeches and Writings* (Cleveland and New York: World, 1946), pp. 24–28.
10. Hoyt Trowbridge, "Aristotle and the 'New Criticism'," *The Sewanee Review*, LII (October 1944), 537–555. See Robert Gorham Davis, "The New Criticism and the Democratic Tradition," *The American Scholar*, XIX (Winter 1949), 9–19.
11. Yvor Winters, "Robert Frost: or, The Spiritual Drifter as Poet," *The Sewanee Review*, LVI (Autumn 1948), 566.
12. *Ibid.*, pp. 586–587. I cannot accept this appraisal of Frost, but the fact that we may be wrong in our judgments does not, of course, relieve us from the responsibility of attempting evaluation.
13. Richard Hofstadter, *The American Political Tradition and the*

74 ROBERT D. CLARK

Men Who Made It (New York: Vintage Books, 1951), pp. 68–92.

14. Robert Merton, *Mass Persuasion: The Social Psychology of a War Bond Drive* (New York: Harper, 1946), pp. 185–188.

15. William Norwood Brigance, "Jeremiah S. Black," in *A History and Criticism of American Public Address,* I, W. N. Brigance, ed. (New York: McGraw-Hill, 1943), pp. 459–482.

16. Wayne Shumaker, *Elements of Critical Theory* (Berkeley and Los Angeles: University of California Press, 1952), pp. 1–13.

Burkeian Criticism

MARIE HOCHMUTH NICHOLS

"More than most other contemporary critics, Kenneth Burke has attempted to draw us back to the fullest meaning of the art with which we are concerned and to find methods and analytical tools that will get at the full resources of the art." *In the following essay Professor Nichols discusses the fundamental assumptions on which Burke's critical method is based.*

Marie Hochmuth Nichols is Professor of Speech at the University of Illinois. Her article is reprinted from the original Western Speech *symposium.*

In his recently published book, *Critical Approaches to Literature,* the English literary critic and scholar, David Daiches, remarks: "There is no single 'right' method of handling literary problems, no single approach to works of literary art that will yield all the significant truths about them." [1] Whereas many rhetorical critics would agree with the assertion in reference to their own endeavors, their practice, we believe, would not lend strong support. A glance at our critical works would indicate an overwhelming number solidly established in conventional aspects of the Aristotelian tradition, with a stress upon the functional and dynamic character of rhetoric. It is true, of course, that an occasional critic has broken through the conventional pattern of criticism to make use of methods deriving from the social psychologists, or again, to apply recommendations deriving from anthropologists or sociologists.

In an era whose emphasis has been on process, not theory, perhaps we may be expected to continue in well-known paths rather than to carve out other paths. Our modern textbooks have removed us so far from the speculative and humane tradition that a major publisher has recently seen fit to observe with reference to a projected book in the humane tradition:

> Although we are in sympathy with your focusing on a liberal arts objective, we wonder how much success you will have in convincing . . . teachers that this is the right approach. . . . If their concentration is in Speech, will they be equipped . . . to succeed with your approach.

Rhetoric as technique designed to secure effects, not rhetoric as an art sustained in and through dialectic, has been our concern, and our lack of equipment to deal with rhetoric in its philosophical aspects has manifested itself in our criticism. The Aristotelian rhetoric read out of the context of the Aristotelian rationale has, of course, made easy the practice of seizing upon the mechanical aspects of the lore.

Cavalier injunctions in some of our modern textbooks have provided further reason for not taking either rhetorical construction or rhetorical criticism seriously. We are enjoined by a modern linguist to *Leave Your Language Alone*. "The merit of what a person says . . . is not affected in any way by the way in which they say it." [2] A textbook writer tells us: "Don't worry too much about the exact meaning of words. . . . In a speech those exact meanings may be lost entirely." [3] The same author in telling how to build a unit of a speech, remarks: "Yes, quote Socrates, Plato, Marcus Aurelius, Cato, Homer—any known person who lived long ago. Few in the audience will know the quotation you select, so you can change it a bit to prove your point." [4] Undaunted by the assertion of modern philosophers that "At the point of the abstract ultimate what is said . . . and the way it is said

. . . may be the same thing," [5] the authors of textbooks sometimes so conceive the rhetorical art as to make unnecessary any serious consideration of it. At our conventions, we sometimes jauntily prate about teaching *practical* speechmaking and of encouraging *practical* criticism as if others might be teaching *impractical* speech-making and encouraging *impractical* criticism. The meaning of practical does not become clearer by the application of labels of virtue. It may be quite possible that one man of solid judgment, bringing enlightenment through an emphasis on the theoretical, is doing more practical criticism and teaching than all the disciples of formulary rhetoric and a rhetoric of gimmicks, put together. Nevertheless, serious critics would be foolish, indeed, to bring the heavy artillery of a full blown critical methodology to products lightly conceived.

More than most other contemporary critics, Kenneth Burke has attempted to draw us back to the fullest meaning of the art with which we are concerned and to find methods and analytical tools that will get at the full resources of the art. It is true, of course, that others have given valiant support to the effort. Maurice Natanson in "The Limits of Rhetoric," [6] Richard Weaver in *The Ethics of Rhetoric*,[7] Donald Bryant in "Rhetoric: Its Function and Its Scope," [8] and others are among these. Perhaps the fountainhead for much of the current endeavor is to be found in Burke, who, for more than thirty years, has sought a re-approachment of rhetoric, dialectic, and ethics. He has had both the literary critics and the rhetorical critics at heart in his efforts.[9]

As a philosopher, he has been searching for the assumptions on which the art rests, assumptions pertaining to language, the nature of meaning, the function of language in producing co-operation, the meaning of persuasion. As a critic, he has searched for a critical methodology appropriate to his rationale.

It is undoubtedly true that the difficulty of Burke's works has prevented a number of potential users of his writings from making practical use of them. Burke is not bed-side reading; nor can a superficial skimming of his works be productive. A few catch phrases or ideas taken from one or another of his works, without reference to fundamental assumptions and qualifications, can only serve to maim and distort.

Although the notion of language using as an *act* is fundamentally Aristotelian, it is a bit of Aristotelianism that has rarely, if ever, received the emphasis given it by Burke. It becomes the basis of his philosophical position and the basis of his critical methodology. It paves the way for a substantive rhetoric rather than a rhetoric of techniques.

In the *Journal of General Education* for April, 1951, under the title "Rhetoric—Old and New," Burke remarks: "If I had to sum up in one word the difference between the 'old' rhetoric and a 'new' (a rhetoric reinvigorated by fresh insights which the 'new sciences' contributed to the subject), I would reduce it to this: The key term for the old rhetoric was 'persuasion' and its stress was upon deliberate design. The key term for the 'new' rhetoric would be *identification,* which can include a partially unconscious factor in appeal." [10] The doctrine of "identification" introduces one of the most troublesome concepts of philosophers for generations. It in turn poses a problem for critics. Burke is concerned with the principle on which appeal rests. In Burke's language, when one "identifies" himself with someone else or something else, he becomes *consubstantial* with it. "A doctrine of *consubstantiality* either explicit or implicit may be necessary to any way of life," [11] says Burke. "For substance in the old philosophies, was an *act;* and a way of life is an *acting-together,* and in acting together, men have common sensations, concepts, images, ideas, attitudes that make them *consubstantial.*" [12]

Now, the word *substance* is not unfamiliar to most of us. The language of everyday speech will yield an unsettling array of uses of it. Doctors speak of a foreign substance in the blood. The politician may say: "The substance of the matter is so and so." And the schoolmen will say, "Professor Osgood's theory of language is substantially the same as that of Charles Morris." If you look into Aristotle, you will find, among other things, that a stone is a substance. If you look in Spinoza you will find only God is a substance. In the main, perhaps, the ancients used the term to denote the indestructible, enduring identity in things, that which is the same in their changing forms and in the differences of their manifestations. Emmanuel Kant who ruled it out of metaphysics found a place for it in our experiences, that is, in our knowledge of the physical world. He included it among his categories as a "necessary form of the mind," like the ideas of time, number, community, causality, etc. When Jeremy Bentham sought to carve off the accretions of language, he discarded all of Aristotle's categories as fictions, retaining only "substance," a category that pertained to a definable entity.

In the first place, then, the term involves the idea of identity, uniqueness. One might ask the question: What is a society? A person who accepts the doctrine of substance would not be satisfied if someone answered: It's an aggregate of people. He would insist that there is a unity of idea or a principle which gives coherence to the parts. Someone might ask, "What is a cell?" and receive the answer, "Well, it's a mass of protoplasm." But a substance thinker would say, "No, the substance of a cell is not protoplasmic stuff but the law according to which the cell divides, re-forms, and divides again."

Curiously enough, as Locke and others before him pointed out, etymologically the word means *to stand under;* hence, it involves a paradox of thinking of a thing both in terms of what it is in itself and what it is extrinsically. For instance, a child both is and is not one with its parents. It is both part of and separate from its parents. Even while it is consubstantial with its parents, it is at the same time a distinct substance in its own right, surrounding itself with properties of its own.

The question now arises: How does the doctrine of substance work out rhetorically and critically? One may suppose that a speaker decides to praise the common man, a distinct substance. The common man has got himself identified with

Communism. Thus, one may identify himself with the common man as the principle of stability and solid virtue, but fail to identify himself with a belief in a given system of property. Or, suppose a speaker decides to praise the Salk solution, a distinct substance. The Salk solution is a product of science, and science has got itself connected with germ warfare. In other words, every distinct substance participates in a wide range of activity. Identification is a word which covers the whole range of activity. A shepherd as shepherd acts for the good of the sheep; in which case one may identify himself with the shepherd's goodness, but the shepherd, in turn, identifies himself with a project, that is raising sheep for the black market, in which case one may cease to identify himself. The notion of substance has a wide range, indeed. It may move around between idealistic and materialistic frames of reference. For instance, if men are separate in body, then show them they are united in spirit. If one wants to sanction a nation's extension of physical dominion, an audience may be made to identify itself with a nation's spreading ideals. If an organization is in disarray, one may talk of its common purposes. If there is a struggle over the means for accomplishing something, one may identify an audience with ends.

Identification may take place in principle or through the whole range of properties and interests with which things get themselves connected. It is grounded in both man's biological nature and in his rational nature. Persuasion involves communication by the signs of consubstantiality.

Although identification appears to take place from the grounding of language in property, one must not lose sight of the fact that, according to Burke, language has a property or resource of its own. Although words are aspects of a wide communicative context, much of which is not verbal at all, yet words have their own peculiar property and peculiarity. One may ask, "What is this nature of their own that words have?" Burke would argue that language at a minimum is a mode of *transcension;* hence, it has dialectical resources in itself and of itself, thus grounding appeal in dialectic. To see the dialectical feature one might note the character of such words and combinations as Albert Einstein, scientist, son of God. What such naming means is that language has the capacity to keep men apart as separate substances, like Albert Einstein, Enrico Fermi, John Locke, but also unite them on the level of idea, "men of science," and round out the symmetry of union on an even higher level of abstraction, "sons of God." This would account for some of the mystical unions and identifications which are brought about whereby men identify themselves with God in ultimate union.

For the critic, Burke's rationale necessitates a system of classification, a naming of manoeuvers that are operating in any language situation, bringing about either by calculation or by "unconscious" appeal, social cohesion, that is, *consubstantiality,* material or idealistic. It requires constant attention to both the biological and rational grounding of appeal. Burke's critical tool for locating the constituents of a situation is variously named, "dramatistic pentad," or "dialectical substance." This five-pronged approach operates to locate in Act, Scene, Agent, Agency, and Purpose the integrated pattern of any experience, and to trace out the location in which identifications are possible. When graduate students coyly ask, "Have you used Burke's pentad for your analysis?" often they are unaware that the pentad is not a gadget that can be separated from the whole Burkeian rationale. What Maurice Natanson complains of in regard to the use of the obvious Aristotelian "techniques," as if they were the whole of the Aristotelian system, is applicable here.[13] To apply Burkeian methodology without reference to the rationale out of which it grows inevitably produces results which are not worth the effort.

The charge, however, that Burke's method is intuitive and that it works for him, but not easily, if at all, for anyone else is, in part, refuted by the successful application of the method by Virginia Holland to Wendell Phillips' "Murder of Lovejoy" address.[14] That the method requires full understanding of Burke's rationale cannot be doubted. That it also requires breadth of background and steady concentration on the various aspects of any situation under consideration in order to see the full working of the elements cannot easily be doubted either. However, the successful application of the tool provides a unity and substance in critical results, often lacking in many of our efforts. For example, the whole of Hitler's *Mein Kampf* can be briefly brought to focus by the use of methodology.[15] Burke's own application of the method results in findings that can be sharply summarized in the following way:

ACT: Bastardization of religious thought.

AGENT: Hitler.

AGENCY: Unity identifications, such as "one voice," Reich, Munich, Army, German democracy, race, nation, Aryan heroism, etc. *vs.* Disunity identifications, such as images, ideas, etc., of parliamentary wrangle of the Habsburgs, Babel of opinion, Jewish cunning, together with spiritualization and materialization techniques.

PURPOSE: Unification of the German people.

SCENE: Discordant elements in a culture weakened progressively by capitalistic materialism.

Burke's theory is best adjusted to the mind willing to continue to inquire, to experiment, to deepen insights with knowledge deriving from a variety of sources. He will not help those interested in preserving tradition for tradition's sake, those interested in partisan loyalties, those interested in formula. Burke would "use all there is to use."

It is in spirit, not merely in method, that Burke is forward looking, even as he makes use of the solid lore of the past. When the modern critic, R. P. Blackmur, differentiated himself from Burke, he observed: "Mr. Burke legislates; I would judge; the executive is between us." [16] For the critic of public address interested in "effects" only, Burke is of little help. If, on the other hand, he wants to get himself inside a speech and find out what is happening, he might find enormous assistance. The legislator is on the floor of the House, in the scramble, aware of internal manoeuvers. Resolutions, or strategies, are shaped by the scramble. The verbalizing is supported by non-verbal activity. The legislator sizes up situations in an effort to encompass them; he makes deals, sometimes with his own conscience, sometimes with constituents. He is attuned to the tonalities of adversaries that he might bring them to willing co-operation. "I was once a farm boy myself," he will say to his adversary in order to establish a bond or to bring about identification or to make two separate identities substantially one. He names things; he takes sides in accordance with truth or in accordancy with expediency; he shifts ground. The president or executive may or may not put his law into action; the court may or may not declare his act unconstitutional. Nevertheless, he has done a necessary and fundamental piece of work.

No modern critic has done more to make meaningful the opening words of the Aristotelian Rhetoric: "Rhetoric is the counterpart of Dialectic." No modern critic has done more to counteract the superficial concern with "personality" as providing the ethical aspect of speech. With the *word* considered to be an *act* in the full moral sense, Burke has called back the ethical foundations of rhetoric from its source in the Aristotelian *Ethics*. "The origin of action," says Aristotle, "its efficient, not its final cause—is choice, and that of choice is desire and reasoning with a view to an end. This is why choice cannot exist either without reason and intellect or without a moral state; for good action and its opposite cannot exist without a combination of intellect and character." [17] Embedded in the concept of *act,* as differentiated from *motion,* lies an ethical concept—language is moral in its basis; it contains the choices, feelings, attitudes of originators. It has dialectical dimension in that it contains in itself the property of transcension, the capacity to separate and unite, name and divide. What language is, not merely what one does with it deliberately, furnishes the real basis for communication—and language above all else is a weighted, socialized medium, serving to unite or separate.

Burke's is a substantive rhetoric, not a rhetoric of techniques, although he does not omit techniques altogether. He treats a speech as a full moral act, grounded in man's biological and rational nature, living in and through dialectic. His critical methodology is based on this assumption; hence, the accuracy of the label "dialectical substance" to the integrated methodology of the "dramatistic pentad"; hence, also *identification* as the key word in his rhetorical system. Critics attempting to apply his system would do well to regard these matters.

NOTES

1. David Daiches, *Critical Approaches to Literature* (New York: Prentice-Hall, 1956), p. 391.
2. Robert A. Hall, Jr., *Leave Your Language Alone* (Ithaca: Cornell University Press, 1950), p. 236.
3. Edward J. Hegarty, *How to Write a Speech* (New York: McGraw-Hill, 1951), pp. 55–56.
4. *Ibid.,* p. 64.
5. E. Jordan, *Essays in Criticism* (Chicago: University of Chicago Press, 1952), p. 193.
6. Maurice Natanson, "The Limits of Rhetoric," *Quarterly Journal of Speech,* XLI (April 1955), 133–139.
7. Richard M. Weaver, *The Ethics of Rhetoric* (Chicago: Henry Regnery, 1953).
8. Donald C. Bryant, "Rhetoric: Its Function and Its Scope," *Quarterly Journal of Speech,* XXXIX (December 1953), 401–424.
9. Kenneth Burke, "The Criticism of Criticism," *Accent,* XV (Autumn 1955), 279–292.
10. Kenneth Burke, "Rhetoric–Old and New," *The Journal of General Education,* V (April 1951), 203.
11. Kenneth Burke, *A Rhetoric of Motives* (New York: Prentice-Hall, 1950), p. 21.
12. *Ibid.*
13. Natanson, *op. cit.,* pp. 133–139.
14. Virginia Holland, "Rhetorical Criticism: A Burkeian Method," *Quarterly Journal of Speech,* XXXIX (December 1953), 444–450.
15. Kenneth Burke, *The Philosophy of Literary Form* (Baton Rouge: Louisiana State University Press, 1941), pp. 191–220.
16. R. P. Blackmur, *Language As Gesture* (New York: Harcourt, Brace, 1952), p. 4.
17. Aristotle, *Ethica Nicomachea,* VI, trans., W. D. Ross (London: Humphrey Milford, 1915), p. 1139a.

Interpretive
Function of the Critic

THOMAS R. NILSEN

Critical evaluation of speeches has tended to focus on the speaker's explicit objectives and his means of achieving them. In this essay the view is presented that a vital function of criticism is the interpreting *of speeches—revealing the concept of man, of ideas, and of society implied by the discourse— so that their meaning and their significance for man and society can be more clearly seen.*

Thomas R. Nilsen is Associate Professor of Speech at the University of Washington. This article is revised from the original Western Speech *symposium.*

The ultimate goal of literary criticism has been stated broadly as *"the full, evaluated apprehension of the critical subject matter."* [1] This goal does not seem to have been considered appropriate for rhetorical criticism. As one writer observed, after quoting Cleanth Brooks to the effect that the function of criticism is "to put the reader in possession of the work of art," this concept of purpose "is not particularly helpful to the rhetorical critic since speeches are seldom abstruse or esoteric (as poems and novels sometimes are). A speech by its very nature is, or should be, immediately comprehensible; hence the interpretative function of the critic is seldom paramount." [2] Whether we agree with this or not depends upon what we mean by "the full, evaluated apprehension of," or being "in possession of." If the meaning of a speech is thought of as the response it explicitly seeks to evoke, then, to be sure, no interpretation is necessary. But if within the meaning of the speech are included the many attendant responses, the more subtle understandings and conceptions evoked by the speech and their possible consequences, then interpretation is a much needed function of the speech critic.

It is the purpose of this paper to urge that a vital function of speech criticism should be to interpret the meaning of speeches, not in the sense of clarifying what the speaker directly intends but in the sense of what the speech indirectly implies, for man and the society in which he lives. This is a complex task, and we can only suggest a few lines of thought that might be followed in making such an interpretation.

Before discussing this conception of criticism we should remind ourselves of the function of that which is being criticized. What then, is the function of the speaker? The literary critic Allen Tate opens a recent essay with these words: "To the question, What should the man of letters be in our time, we should find the answer in what we need him to do." [3] Now we do not have "speakers" in the sense that we have writers, but there are many men whose duty and some whose inclination leads them into the role of speakers. A question like Allen Tate's seems germane. What should the speaker be or do in our time? And the answer should lie in what we need him to do. We need him, ultimately, to move men to acts that fulfill men. Indeed, it has always been the speaker's function to move men; but in our time, with its extraordinary complexities and its confusing lack of common values, it is more than ever necessary to inquire into how the speaker is moving men and to what ends. A pervasive concern with human ends is characteristic of our age. As summarized in a phrase by Lewis Mumford, this concern is felt in the area of rhetoric as everywhere else: "We must bring to every activity and every plan a new criterion of judgment: we must ask how far it seeks to further the processes of life fulfillment and how much respect it pays to the needs of the whole personality." [4] In a broad sense this is the meaning of a speech for man and society, and inquiry into such meaning is the task of the critic.

When urging this task upon the critic we must be clear on the sense in which the term "ends" is being used. It would seem obvious that the critic would go rather far afield if he were to pass judgment on the rightness or wrongness of the terminal action sought by a speech unless such action might have a bearing on the processes of democracy, such as an infringement on the rights of free speech or assembly. Whether to raise or lower tariffs, whether to build a public or private dam in some river gorge, whatever his personal convictions on these issues, as a speech critic these should not be his concern. The end or effect of primary concern to the speech critic is the pattern of attitudes and thought processes induced by the speech, particularly in relation to the terminal action it seeks to elicit. It must be plain that in a democratic society the *process* of reaching a decision is often, if not generally, more important than the decision itself. The critic should be vitally interested in the effect of a speech, but his interest should be mainly in what we might call the intermediate effect, the method of decision, the pattern of thought and action to which men are moved by the speech.

The question of *how* the speaker moves his listeners is traditionally a question for rhetorical criticism. The selection and organization of ideas, the choice of words, and the delivery are evaluated in light of the purpose the speaker seeks to achieve. When, however, we view as the concern of the critic not only the terminal action explicitly sought, but also the method of decision entailed, the analysis of the *how* takes on an added dimension. It is then not only a problem of discovering rhetorical factors and discerning how they function to achieve the stated purpose of the speech, but also discerning how rhetorical factors contribute to a way of thinking about and of doing that which is called for in the speech. Evaluating how well the speaker uses rhetorical techniques to accomplish his purpose is certainly an important task of the critic, but no less important—more so, no doubt—is an evaluation of the pattern of thought and action fostered by the speech. The latter, usually indirectly communicated, stems from the sense of values the speech embodies, the values it attaches to man himself, to his ideas, to his relationships with other men. And this gives us a cue to the critical analyses of speeches. The rhetorical techniques, the means of persuasion, are the speaker's response to the rhetorical needs of a particular situation, but as such they are also a reflection of the speaker's concept of man, in what he asks him to do and how; his concept of ideas, in what he presents and the manner in which he develops it; his concept of society, in what he implies about the relationship of man to man. These are the things of enduring significance about a speech which the critic must reveal if the meaning of the speech is to be made plain, if we are to be put in any real sense in "possession" of the speech.

To interpret the meaning of a speech, in the sense suggested here, how might the critic view man, ideas, and society, and what questions might he ask about the speech? Let us consider each of the concepts in turn and suggest a possible approach to this type of critical analysis.

The concept of man. To refer again to Allen Tate, he says further of the writer that "he must recreate for his age the image of man, and he must propagate standards by which other men may test that image, and distinguish the false from the true." [5] If we leave to the writer the task of recreating for his age the image of man, we must nonetheless ask the speaker what his image of man is, for upon this will depend how he believes men should choose and act. "A theory of human nature," as T. R. Jessop has put it, "irrespective of whether it be true or false, is never merely a concept or an image, but it is an active force, shaping, reshaping or misshaping the mind that holds it. A man's life contracts or widens as his belief about himself and others becomes narrow or large." [6]

The speaker himself may never have clearly seen his own image of man; he may never have made articulate his assumptions about man. It becomes the critic's function to reveal what manner of man the speaker sees in his listeners, so that they may distinguish the false from the true. The concept of man is not, of course, to be determined by the speaker's explicit assertions or protestations. It is easy enough—and imperative in public life—to pay lip service to man as created in the image of God, but it is another thing to have the full implications of the speech bear out this image. The speaker's concept of man is reflected in the manner in which he speaks, the language he employs, the information he presents or fails to present, the issues he chooses, the questions he raises, the faiths he generates, the doubts he implies, the feelings he appeals to, the process of choice he inspires.

Specifically, in revealing the concept of man we should need to ask such questions as these: Does the speech reveal an image of man as a being of intrinsic worth, or of one whose worth as a personality derives from possessions, characteristics, or creed? Is the image of man that of a being with a capacity for wisdom and rational choice, the exercise of whose rationality in the light of growing wisdom it is the speaker's obligation to encourage? Men do not fulfill themselves by being moved like pawns or bishops no matter how laudable the acts they perform when thus moved. They become better men when their acts are self-determined (in so far as their human nature allows), based on rational informed choice, with adequate consideration for other men. "Whether it be in the field of individual or social activity," wrote Alexander Meiklejohn, "men are not recognizable as men unless, in any given situation, they are using their minds to give direction to their behavior." [7]

Does a speech deal honestly with men? Does it realistically relate them to the problems they face or does it raise spurious alarm or spurious complacency? Does the speech imply that men must grow in understanding of themselves and the world about them or that they should forsake the dangers of thought for the safety of convention? Does the speech falsely flatter men to their immediate gratification but long term peril? The problem of intellectual honesty is particularly significant since it is in part, at least, a function of the democratic concept of man. This is pointed up in an observation on political speaking by Alan Valentine:

> As popular sovereignty developed politicians found it expedient to proclaim the political competence of the average American, and assure him that he was at least as good as anyone else. Even his cultural limitations were exalted to political virtues; his very averageness became moral superiority; his untrained mind was translated into a treasury of basic Wordsworthian wisdom, undefiled by patrician sophistries.[8]

Such exaltation of limitations hardly inspires intellectual or emotional growth, a thoughtful and sober approach to social problems, or a sensitive awareness of one's responsibilities to other men.

Further, does the speech encourage respect for the spirit of free men? To quote again from Valentine (whose strictures on this age of conformity imply so much about our concept of man):

> Any American has the right to try to persuade others to adopt his way of thought, for persuasion is the essence of democracy. But he must use no methods, legal or illegal, contrary to the spirit of free men. To go beyond pure persuasion by threatening or hinting some social or economic penalty for failure to accept the general philosophy, is to offend that spirit.[9]

The concept of ideas. The speaker's concept of ideas is, of course, inseparable from his concept of man. How he uses ideas will depend upon how he believes men should choose and act. Perhaps the basic consideration is whether through the manipulation of ideas the speaker will determine what his hearers shall think and do, or through his creative use of ideas his hearers will be helped to decide and do for themselves. Max Lerner has sharply revealed this contrast in speaking of ideas as being used *instrumentally* or *manipulatively:*

> If you use ideas instrumentally your primary regard is for their validity, and for the creative action they will evoke through that validity, and for the social action that will result. If you view them manipulatively, your only regard is for the use you can make of them. They become instruments not for creativeness but for contrivance.[10]

The essential question is this: Does the speech present ideas so that they take on added meaning, so that they relate to other significant ideas, so that the listener can see the world a little more as a whole and can use his own intelligence more effectively than before, or does the speech perpetuate narrow meanings, isolate ideas, avoid critical appraisal, and use ideas as pushbuttons to trigger off preselected responses?

Of course, the limitations of public address as a medium for dealing with ideas must be recognized. The truth is often complicated, and the time of a speech is short. Few audiences can or will follow closely reasoned discourse. Simple alternatives, personality conflicts, dramatized hopes and fears are enormously appealing. Critical judgment must be made with full allowance for such limitations. But it still can be expected that the speaker will use his medium to the limits of its capacity. It is not just a matter of what the speaker does with an idea, but what he fails to do. The difference between what he might do in a given case and what he actually does is a measure of his failure.

The concept of society. Our interest in man and society stems from the fact that man fulfills himself only in a social context, through his interactions, direct and indirect, with other men. We are thinking of society here as a set of relationships among people, a pattern of interactions among men, that remains more or less stable. We do not conceive of such a set of relationships as an end in itself, but rather as a means to an end, the end being the fulfillment of man. The critic must reveal what concept of society the speech reflects; for this reveals how the speaker believes men should choose and act, how he would have them fulfill themselves. Again, we cannot judge the speaker's concept of society by his explicit professions of belief. It seems apparent that many men in public life who speak of democracy have a very inadequate understanding of what it involves, of the method of choice and the principles of action it requires. Moreover, the speaker may never have attempted to clarify and articulate his own thinking about what is fundamental to the democratic process. The speaker's concept of society must be seen in the values the speech embodies and the social processes it promotes.

When we accept as an area of serious inquiry and instruction free public address and the criticism thereof, we have already assumed the desirability if not the necessity of a democratic society. Without a democratic society we cannot have free public address, and without free public address at once to express and continuously recreate its values we cannot have democracy. The critic's inquiry into the concept of society is fundamentally an inquiry into what the speech implies about the democratic values we have assumed essential to man's most adequate fulfillment of himself. But democracy is a complex thing, and it is possible to hold different views of its essential character. If democracy is to be a concern of the speech critic the vital relationship must be seen between public address and the basic values of a democratic society. Such a relationship can be suggested by contrasting two views of democracy, one which sees its basic values as "substantive," the other which sees them as "procedural." The substantive view is provided by John Hallowell:

> True freedom requires both knowledge of the good and the will to choose the good when known. The denial of either is the denial of freedom, and the denial of freedom is the rejection of that moral agency in man which characterizes his humanity. . . . The preservation of freedom demands that we recover our faith both in the ability of man to know the good and in his capacity, within the limitations of historical conditioning and the defectiveness of his will, to choose the good when known.[11]

The procedural view is suggested by Kurt Tauber:

> Liberal democracy is primarily characterized by its emergence as an open, pluralistic society, that is, which rests upon the primacy of the values of rationality, tolerance, and the moral autonomy of the individual. . . . The values of an open society are not so much substantive as methodological or procedural. . . . It is not contempt for the "truth" that assures victory to the idolatry of "falsehood," but the contempt for reason and the open society that loses the battle to the irrationalism of the tribe. The problem of the open society is not the problem of error, but the problem of intolerance, of limiting the area of free inquiry, free criticism, and free choice.[12]

These views are not mutually exclusive, but they do reveal significantly differing conceptions of democracy that are important to the speech critic. If one sees as the critic's business the assessment of the effects of a speech in the sense of the terminal action evoked, then there would appear to be implied an acceptance of the substantive view of democracy, that is, the assumption of the capacity to judge what is right or wrong in accordance with moral law. But if one sees the effects that are of concern to the critic as the intermediate effects, that is, the method of choice and principles of action engendered, then acceptance of the procedural view would seem to be implied. The speech critic could conceivably take either position; but it is the view taken here that since the procedures of democracy involve the function of speech in its various forms, the procedural values are of unique concern to the speech critic. Men can differ on many substantive values, on whether particular acts are right or wrong, and still live and work together constructively in a democratic society; but they cannot differ widely on procedures and so live and work together. As Walter Lippmann put it some years ago, "There is but one kind of unity possible in a world as diverse as ours. It is unity of method rather than of aim. . . ." [13] Or to use John Hallowell's words, "If men are to unite it must be in terms of principles rather than in terms of interests." [14] It is our agreement to follow certain procedural principles in achieving our varied interests that makes democracy possible. It is these procedural principles, in so far as they involve or are affected by public address, that are a prime concern of the speech critic.

Seeking to understand the implications for society embodied in the speech, its impact on democratic procedures, we should ask what the speech implies about rationality, tolerance, and the moral autonomy of the individual; what it implies about the expression of opinions, deliberation and persuasion, free inquiry, free criticism, and free choice; what it implies about discussion and debate, the use of information, the interchange of ideas, the function of opposition, and attitudes toward what is orthodox and unorthodox in thought and action. Only if what the speech implies about these attitudes and procedures is made clear, can we make significant judgments about the ends to which the speech is moving men.

Speeches are designed to have an effect upon the hearers, usually in the form of an act to be committed or a belief to be accepted. In addition, speeches inevitably foster a way of acting and a way of believing. It is the view presented here that it is the function of the speech critic to reveal the way of acting and believing fostered by the speech and the possible conse-

quences thereof. This is the more significant meaning of the
speech for the society upon which it has its impact, and this
meaning is primarily to be seen in the concept of man, the
concept of ideas, and the concept of society embodied in the
speech.

NOTES

1. Wayne Shumaker, *Elements of Critical Theory* (Berkeley and Los Angeles: University of California Press, 1952), p. 13.
2. Barnet Baskerville, "The Critical Method in Speech," *Central States Speech Journal,* IV (July 1953), 2.
3. Allen Tate, *The Man of Letters in the Modern World* (New York: Meridian Books, 1955), p. 11.
4. Lewis Mumford, *The Condition of Man* (New York: Harcourt, Brace, 1944), p. 423.
5. Tate, *op. cit.,* p. 11.
6. T. E. Jessop, *The Freedom of the Individual in Society* (Toronto: Ryerson Press, 1948), p. 31.
7. Alexander Meiklejohn, *Free Speech and Its Relation to Self-Government* (New York: Harpers, 1948), p. 6.
8. Alan Valentine, *The Age of Conformity* (Chicago: Henry Regnery, 1954), p. 37.
9. *Ibid.,* p. 63.
10. Max Lerner, *Ideas Are Weapons* (New York: Viking Press, 1940), p. 11.
11. John H. Hallowell, *The Moral Foundation of Democracy* (Chicago: University of Chicago Press, 1954), pp. 112–113.
12. Kurt P. Tauber, "The Free University in an Open Society," *The Harvard Educational Review,* XXIII (Winter 1953), 4–7.
13. Walter Lippmann, *Liberty and the News* (New York: Harcourt, Brace and Howe, 1920), p. 67.
14. Hallowell, *op. cit.,* p. 55.

Extrinsic and Intrinsic Criticism

W. CHARLES REDDING

The problems of extrinsic and intrinsic criticism of literary texts have their counterparts in the criticism of rhetorical discourse. The inadequacy of an exclusively historical approach to a study of texts is felt among rhetorical critics, says Professor Redding, as it has been among literary critics. He presents content analysis as an important technique for the study—the intrinsic criticism—of speeches.

W. Charles Redding is Professor and Director of the Communication Research Center of the Department of Speech of Purdue University. His article is revised from the original Western Speech *symposium.*

As he contemplated the state of literary scholarship some years ago, Norman Foerster was impelled to remark that "the inclination of scholars to move out of rather than more deeply into their own subject is a symptom of a dubious state of affairs in their own subject." [1] Literary scholars, he felt, had abandoned their true calling by immersing themselves in research which dealt with such matters as sources, textual validity, allusions, biography, psychology, social environment, historical data—with everything, that is, but analysis and criticism of the literary texts themselves. Analogies are notoriously vulnerable as logical instruments; but if construed only as suggestive similarities, they can be useful. What is here proposed is a scrutiny of popular methods of rhetorical criticism, focused upon certain issues that may be as relevant for public address as for literature. In short, this question is asked: Is it possible that rhetorical scholars have too often moved out of rather than more deeply into their own subject?

The Magna Carta for rhetorical critics, now become a classic, was embodied in a brilliant essay by H. A. Wichelns, published in 1925.[2] Although our professional charter appeared only about four decades ago, already there has developed something approaching an orthodoxy of method in the criticism of public address. Indeed, we were told in 1949 that rhetorical criticism had by that date attained "a stage of maturity" and that its "methodology has become fairly well standardized and accepted."[3] Despite many evidences of discontent and years of discussion, there is good reason to believe that the situation in 1966 is not radically different—at least for the great majority of doctoral students—than it was in 1949.

Stated most briefly, this "standard" methodology can be characterized as an application of rhetorical criteria to materials derived from historical research. Most of it has been focused upon the speaker, and most of it "has followed the traditional patterns of investigation employed in history, biography, and literature."[4] As A. C. Baird has described the evolution of method in rhetorical criticism, there was at first a period in which directors of research groped for valid tools and explored all the well-known approaches—including the survey, the experimental, and the quantitative. What finally prevailed was "a combination of the historical-literary-rhetorical methods" applied to the "evaluation of outstanding speakers"; hence, "the critic of speeches and of speakers became [both] a historian and a rhetorician."[5]

The most significant feature of this methodology, derived from Wichelns' analysis of public address as a speaker-audience event, has been its heavy reliance upon historical data and historical research techniques. An examination of published research tends to support F. L. Whan's judgment of twenty years ago that rhetorical scholarship has been dominantly "historical in nature," [6] and Bower Aly's assertion that "the biographical approach to American oratory has been the most thoroughly developed." [7] There may be two chief reasons accounting for this historical-biographical emphasis—the first political, and the second doctrinal. The political reason was well expressed by Wayne Thompson when he suggested that while "speech departments were struggling to attain an academic position equal to that of departments of English, history, and mathematics," it was "probably a matter of good politics" to imitate the work of "better-established fields" and to "make only minor adaptations" of historical and literary methods.[8] The doctrinal reason is the more basic, and the one which concerns us here. It is derived from Hoyt Hudson's definition of rhetoric,[9] a definition applied by Wichelns to the practice of criticism—essentially the Aristotelian view that rhetoric is concerned with persuading an audience. Hence, as Wichelns argued, the rhetorical critic will take a "different attitude toward the orator" (different from that of the literary critic), for he will recognize the unique function of the orator "for what is is: the art of influencing men in some concrete situation." Therefore, the point of view of the rhetorical critic, as Wichelns expounded it, is "patently single"; unlike that of the literary critic, "it is not concerned with permanence, nor yet with beauty." Rather, "it is concerned with effect. It regards speech as a communication to a specific audience, and holds its business to be the analysis and appreciation of the orator's method of imparting his ideas to his hearers." [10]

The rationale of historically oriented criticism, a logical corollary of the focus upon audience effects, is, of course, that speeches can be understood only when studied in the social milieu or setting of which they are an integral part.[11] Reconstruction of past events means, therefore, that the critic must "summon history to the aid of criticism." [12]

It is not suggested here that this rationale lacks cogency.

Certainly there can be no quarrel with the doctrine that if a speech is to be apprehended in its totality, then it must be studied in context—that is, as an event taking place in history, the product of one person communicating with other persons. However, in the balance of this essay it will be suggested that some inferences which apparently have been drawn from this admittedly sound premise may be called into question.

In considering whether Foerster's charge can legitimately be brought against rhetorical critics, we may find it helpful to reexamine exactly what Wichelns was attacking when he rejected the methods of literary criticism. The crucial words in his critique of the literary approach to public address are no doubt "permanence" and "beauty." Then the question becomes: to what extent do these terms refer to the actual research *methodology* of literary scholarship? The answer seems to be that they represent, rather than methods or techniques, a point of view; they are touchstones commonly applied to the evaluation of literary materials. In other words, "permanence" and "beauty" denote *criteria* rather than methods. As such, therefore, they are indeed inappropriate as prime bases upon which to evaluate public address. But they bear no necessary relation to methodology per se. Hence, we should not be surprised that Wichelns himself could admit of rhetorical criticism that "its tools are those of literature." [13] In like vein William Brigance also conceded that "the tools of rhetoric may indeed be the same as those of literature"—even though "the atmosphere and purpose are different." [14] And Donald Bryant has discussed at length the "literary tradition of rhetoric," [15] while reaffirming a few years later his conviction that there was "no need to relocate the field of rhetoric and scholarship as envisioned by Hudson and Wichelns, nor to recant" [16] the views which he himself had first published in 1937 that:

> . . . methods and materials in literary history and critical scholarship apply likewise in oratory and rhetoric. Some modifications and adaptations, of course, are necessary; but we al-

ways have an overlapping so great that method in literary history is almost the same as in rhetorical history.[17]

It should be clear, then, that the revolt proclaimed by Wichelns and his successors has been primarily against criteria rather than methods.

Now, what have been the most important—or at least the most popular—research methods utilized by literary scholars and critics? A bewildering variety of approaches will, of course, be found in the massive corpus of literary scholarship. But there seems little question that the dominant and most widely approved mode of literary study (at least until very recently) has been the historical or philological. It is important to inquire why this has been so.

Departments of literature (that is, "English" in this country), from which speech departments were eventually to spring, became established as academic entities in the late decades of the nineteenth century. For all its so-called romanticism, the nineteenth century was also the century of positivism. It was a century that witnessed the ascendancy of science and technology; it was a century that nurtured Darwin, Pearson, Gibbs, and Peirce; it was a century that worshiped objective "facts." Scholars in the humanities, imbued with the laudable desire to rescue their studies from the vagaries of subjective theorizing, looked to the natural sciences for methods to achieve the fashionable criteria of "objectivity, impersonality, and certainty." [18] Men like von Ranke, Comte, and Taine sought to create scientific history, scientific sociology, and scientific literary criticism. "In an age enormously impressed by the achievements of natural science, and convinced that even literature and the arts must be studied with 'scientific methods,' the historian too had to be 'scientific' at all costs." [19]

The literary scholars, including those who may be called philologists, imported (typically from the German universities) a methodology not of criticism, but of history; and the history was usually of the type recommended by von Ranke, who in 1828 had issued his famous pronouncement of "scientific history." The historian, he said, must write an objective account of things as they really occurred (*"wie es eigentlich gewesen"*). Thus, the historical approach to literature, "made fashionable by the prestige of the natural sciences," helped to perpetuate the identification of "scientific and historical method." [20] Taine set the pattern of historically oriented literary criticism with his canons—*race, moment, milieu*. The result was what René Wellek has called the "common nineteenth-century divorce between literary criticism and history." [21] In other words—and here is the crux of the issue—the literary scholars pursued historical facts so tenaciously that criticism of the literary works themselves was largely ignored or relegated to the limbo of polite essays in the Sunday supplements.

What, then, was the dominant type of literary criticism against which, following the banner raised by Wichelns in 1925, the rhetoricians rebelled? Clearly, it was historical criticism; it emphasized factual research, and, regardless of aesthetic criteria like permanence and beauty, it was typically an extrinsic methodology, that is, it was preoccupied with the surroundings of literature rather than with the literary works themselves. In 1951, an English professor remarked of the contemporary requirements for publication in most research journals that "new factual information is the *sine qua non*," whereas criticism contributing to an understanding of the literary text is at most only a "desirable accessory." [22] And Wayne Shumaker observed in 1952 that "the pages of scholarly journals continue to be filled, for the most part, with studies that depend frankly on external reference frames." [23] Although the situation has changed in a number of respects since 1952, Shumaker's characterization is still a valid description of the long-term trends over several decades of publications.

But now we arrive at what Shumaker has called "one of the central issues of [all] critical theory," namely, "the relative usefulness of external and internal frames." [24] Despite the persisting popularity of extrinsic (or historical) methods, over the years there have been many objectors. Especially during the last two or three decades "a widespread disillusionment with scientific methods" has occurred, resulting in an increasing "use of internal reference frames by large numbers of practicing critics." [25] This modern trend has been epitomized as "a healthy reaction . . . which recognizes that the study of literature should, first and foremost, concentrate on the actual works of art themselves." [26] In fact, Shumaker felt in 1952 that "the partisans of intrinsic analysis are just now strongly entrenched in their positions" and that a new "methodological trend is presently vigorous." [27] As any reader of these pages is no doubt aware, the label commonly applied to the methodological approach based upon "intrinsic analysis" of the literary text is "The New Criticism"—a term impossible of precise definition, but denoting in a general way a point of view promulgated by a heterogeneous group of "philosophers, psychologists, critics, and poets," united (in spite of innumerable individual differences) in their concern "to restore the literary text to its central position amidst a welter of historical-sociological scientism whose data . . . have almost buried it." [28] It is not at all surprising that the reaction embodied in the New Criticism has itself induced a counter-reaction; no doubt John Jellicorse is reporting accurately when he asserts that, in the mid-1960s, many English professors are now "recognizing the sterility of the concepts and methods . . . inherited from New Criticism." [29]

Nevertheless, whether or not the New Criticism turns out to be the wave of the future in literary scholarship, it is indisputable that for years there have been expressions of discontent with the purely historical approach. Admittedly, the inherent character of public address—a communication instrument designed to influence men in a place and in a moment of history—cannot permit a direct application of the New Critics' arguments to rhetorical criticism. Most importantly, the New Criticism is frankly concerned with aesthetics rather than instrumental audience effects. This is obviously not the place to discuss further the intricacies of the New Criticism. But in so far as basic issues are involved, useful analogies appear to exist between the problems of extrinsic criticism of literature and the problems of extrinsic criticism of public address.

To put the matter bluntly, is not some kind of reappraisal in order when samplings of several dozen rhetorical studies published since 1940 reveal that about three-fourths of the space is typically devoted to historical or biographical information, with sometimes as little as one-tenth allotted to detailed analysis of speeches? Other observers have apparently perceived the same phenomenon. As long ago as 1944, commenting primarily upon dissertations in rhetorical criticism, Loren Reid warned against the temptation to write "second-rate history" and "to abandon criticism" by producing "treatises upon politics, religion, historical movements, military strategy, and what not." In 1954 Wayland Parrish advocated a critical method which would focus upon the "quality" of speeches, rather than upon "toting up" audience responses (which he felt to be the historian's task). In 1956 Albert Croft declared, "Most theses following the standard method of rhetorical criticism have done little beyond the writing of political history." Although neither Marie Hochmuth Nichols nor Edwin Black, in their recent books, attacks excessive historicism as such, the thrust of their arguments unquestionably is that rhetorical critics typically slight close analysis of speech content—especially of "style." Douglas Ehninger, reviewing Black's book, is convinced that "even the most gifted of the neo-Aristotelians tend to write history first and rhetorical criticism second, while those with lesser talents write history exclusively." [30]

The traditional view among rhetorical critics, regarded by many as an axiom, has been that public address must be studied and evaluated ultimately in terms of a single overriding criterion: the *effect* of speaking upon specified audiences.[31] In recent years even more practicing critics have begun to question this view. Black's 1965 book, *Rhetorical*

Criticism, represents undoubtedly the most detailed and wide-ranging attack upon the whole "effects" doctrine. Time will be required, of course, to determine whether Ehninger's evaluation is justified: "If . . . Wichelns' landmark essay of 1925 gave neo-Aristotelianism its birth, this book published exactly forty years later . . . may well deal the school its death blow." [32]

Considerations of both space and relevancy preclude an adequate exposition here of the contending positions in this debate.[33] However, it must be noted that, without question, the insistence upon effect as the central concern of rhetorical criticism has had the logical consequence of describing the critic of speeches as "a social historian as well as a biographer." [34] It has been familiar advice to declare that the critic's work "will be sound only when it uses the results of historical study," [35] and that the critic of oratory must "know more history than we can expect the historian to know of oratory." [36] Adoption of the premise that "in many respects the most important constituent of the rhetorical judgment . . . [is] the historical," [37] discouraged rhetorical critics from applying their talents to a truly sophisticated "in depth" analysis of speech content.

In summary, then, it appears that in turning from the admittedly irrelevant aesthetic criteria of literary scholarship, we may have appropriated at the same time two important components of that same scholarship: (1) an excessive preoccupation with historical research, and (2) a derogation of intensive textual analysis (even when reasonably adequate speech texts are available).[38]

What will be suggested here is no abandonment of historical method as an indispensable component of rhetorical scholarship. It would be absurd to argue that the "meanings" in speech content can be understood in a vacuum. Various kinds of extrinsic data—historical, biographical, sociopsychological, economic, cultural—will always be essential (in different proportions as the specific case requires) to anyone who pretends to offer a full understanding of the spoken word. But rhetorical critics will be urged to give careful thought to a shift in emphasis, to seek out precision tools that will enable them to handle the intrinsic aspects of their work as effectively as the extrinsic. The rest of this paper will be devoted to a consideration of ways in which speech content may be analyzed.

Analysis, of course, is conceded to be but one part of the *total* enterprise of criticism (which is, according to Shumaker, the "full, evaluated apprehension of the critical subject").[39] However, there is certainly a place for studies that frankly concentrate upon analysis. As historians and others have long ago discovered, severe limitation of the subject is inescapable if thorough scholarship be the goal: "The necessity of limiting each critical book or essay to some part of the total critical process has been increasingly recognized in recent years," declares Shumaker.[40] And Croft has argued that competent "interpretive or evaluative studies . . . can be managed only on subjects of limited scope," adding that "the time is overdue when doctoral theses in Speech should be less compendious and more thorough" and "the presumption that every graduate student must have a whole new speaker of his own is preposterous." [41] One—but certainly only one—way of limiting the scope of critical studies is to focus upon analysis rather than evaluation as the *primary* goal. It will be argued, and rightly, that analysis and evaluation are never completely separable into neat, mutually exclusive compartments. However, the work of the New Critics in literature and of the content analysts in the social sciences demonstrates that there are practical possibilities for producing research which is dominantly analytic in approach. Once more, rhetorical critics are invited to reflect upon Shumaker's reasoning; in a discussion too complex for summarizing here, he proposes a "dichotomy . . . between evaluative critical statements . . . and analytic or descriptive (nonevaluative) statements" —while readily admitting that any single sentence may contain both elements.[42] Without committing oneself to Shumaker's arguable position, it is possible at least to accept it as a fruitful working hypothesis (while at the same time conceding, with Reid, that the total "critical task is incomplete" if we indulge exclusively in analysis).[43] Analytically oriented studies, for example, can provide empirical evidence for both theoretical and methodological investigations.

It appears that analytic studies may proceed in either of two general directions. First, they may (and typically do) utilize the lore of traditional rhetorical theory; frequently the authors of such studies restrict themselves to identifying examples of various rhetorical canons or "forms" or devices within speech content. This is a conventional approach. Unfortunately, it has too often been little more than a copybook exercise. Although not denying that traditional rhetorical analysis can, in the hands of a perceptive scholar, yield valuable insights, I frankly recommend to all rhetorical critics a careful study of the second direction in which they may move: that of "content analysis" as the term is used in its special and technical sense. In this special sense (which has developed since the early 1940s), content analysis must be differentiated, as Bernard Berelson has warned, from the kind of gross, unsystematic procedure that occurs "whenever someone reads a body of communication content and then [merely] summarizes and interprets what is there"—as, for example, in traditional historical or literary criticism.[44]

Content analysis, as a research technique applicable to the study of public address, is typically a close, sentence-by-sentence (or even word-by-word) scrutiny of oral or written discourse for the purpose of determining what kinds of "meanings" the words may represent. It is really a semantic analysis of symbols (hence the term "symbol-analysis," coined by Harold Lasswell around 1940). It is usually characterized by rather elaborate systematization, with or without precisely defined quantitative units, and with or without mathematical analysis (although the great majority of published studies commonly regarded as examples of content analysis contain varying degrees of quantification—in fact, Berelson insists upon quantification as "perhaps the most distinctive feature of content analysis").[45] It has been called a technique for finding out *"how much* of *what* is *presented how."* [46] Another way of looking at content analysis is to regard it as a means of "putting a wide variety of different word patterns into a single category" [47]—or into many categories. A useful formal definition (although not necessarily accepted by all specialists in the field) is the one offered by Irving Janis:

> . . . any technique (a) for the *classification* of the *sign-vehicles* [i.e., lexical words or equivalent symbols], (b) which relies solely upon the *judgments* (which . . . may range from perceptual discrimination to sheer guesses) of an analyst or group of analysts as to which sign-vehicles fall into which categories, (c) on the basis of *explicitly formulated rules,* (d) provided that the analyst's judgments are regarded as the reports of a *scientific observer.*[48]

It should not be supposed from such definitions that competent content analysis can be executed only with quantitative-mathematical operations. A number of highly regarded nonquantitative studies (sometimes called "qualitative" or "nonfrequency") have been published; notably Leo Lowenthal and Norbert Guterman's analysis of anti-Semitic American "agitators," and Alexander George's ingenious detective work on Nazi war intentions.[49] Moreover, even when quantification is employed (as it is in a majority of instances), simple frequency counts are being supplemented, if not replaced, by such sophisticated procedures as contingency and evaluative assertion analyses.[50]

In fact, the more elementary forms of frequency counts have justly been criticized on the grounds that they provide an imposing and cumbersome machinery for revealing nothing more than would emerge from a perceptive reading of the text by an informed critic. Undeniably, "many studies have an authentic air of busy work about them," [51] and fail to "go beyond the reaffirmation of the obvious." [52]

It would not be possible in this essay, even if it were appropriate, to provide a complete exposition of the detailed procedures employed in a bewildering variety of content analysis methodologies. However, at least four very general kinds of content analysis may be distinguished:

(1) *Qualitative analysis* (also sometimes called nonquantitative, or nonfrequency analysis; Berelson suggests the term "content assessment").[53]

(2) *"Conventional frequency count,"* based in turn upon subjective judgments—or "qualitative identifications." [54]

(3) *Contingency analysis,* although involving quantification and counting, "asks not how often a given symbolic form appears . . . but how often it appears in conjunction with other symbolic units." [55] For example, the analyst may seek to determine whether a speaker's references to "free enterprise" and "progress" are linked together more often, or less often, than chance expectancies would predict. (Charles Osgood emphasizes that, in contrast to much analytical research, the contingency method is particularly useful for making inferences about the mental processes—that is, "the association structure"—of the communicator himself.) [56]

(4) *Evaluative assertion analysis,* a fairly recent development in the field, is designed primarily to yield quantitative indices of the direction ("valence") and the intensity with which the message-sender expresses evaluative attitudes toward whatever "attitude objects" the researcher may specify. It is a complex procedure, one which can be extremely time-consuming; but it is valuable for achieving relative uniformity among coders working as a team.[57] A central feature is the reduction of "raw verbal text" to simplified three-part assertions, each consisting of (1) the specified attitude object, (2) a verbal "connector," and (3) a "complement." Value "weights" (typically 1, 2, or 3) are assigned to the second and third elements, and then multiplied algebraically (for example, $+2$ multiplied by -3, yielding the product -6) to arrive at an evaluative score for each assertion. A summation type of formula is employed to compute a generalized evalu-

ative score for each attitude object, representing the entire communicative unit under study (for example, a speech).

These four kinds of procedures do not exhaust the methodological repertory of contemporary content analysts; for example, there should be added special modifications of "cloze procedure," "Q-sort," and various linguistic devices. The point here is simply that there does exist an impressive array of ingenious analytical tools available for any investigator who earnestly desires to subject the content of public speeches to really exhaustive scrutiny.[58]

Although it is true that content analysis has been developed and applied chiefly by investigators with a behavioral science orientation, and although many rhetorical scholars will not feel comfortable with the more sophisticated experimental and quantitative applications of the method, unquestionably there is virtually unlimited opportunity here for devising appropriate adaptations of the basic rationale to the specific objectives of rhetorical criticism. In fact, some form of content analysis—no matter how subjective or limited in scope—should be of the very essence of rhetorical criticism. Nichols believes a methodological poverty has afflicted many rhetorical critics: "Perhaps we have found wanting our critical approaches to language and style and have not searched seriously for more fruitful methods of analysis." She also feels that methodology as a whole, but particularly methodology for analyzing speech content, is "an area . . . in which we as rhetoricians are notoriously weak," and therefore an area in which rhetorical scholars should be searching for new tools.[59]

To take a single example, it is interesting to note that Black, after commending Martin Maloney for his critique of the speaking of Clarence Darrow, argues that in only one area is Maloney's method questionable ("the critic's one lapse from his otherwise sustained psychological analysis")—the section dealing with "Darrow's persuasive techniques," or, in other words, with the *content* of Darrow's speeches. It is

Black's opinion that this section reveals a "pristine state of this whole approach to rhetorical criticism," characterized by undue reliance upon the traditional concepts of *logos, pathos, ethos,* "patterns of argument," and delivery. Such a treatment, says Black, fails to provide "an entirely satisfactory accounting for the social symbol that Darrow became through his discourse." And then Black proposes a significant diagnosis: "We need not seek far for the reason; we can sense it in the abrupt shift in tone when Maloney approaches the subject of rhetorical techniques. A method for the psychological examination of rhetorical discourse was simply not available to this critic. . . ." [60] In other words, Black seems to be saying that the critic did not find in his rhetorical inventory an apparatus for dealing in depth with speech content.

Whether we wish to accept Black's particular evaluation in this case or not, there can be no disputing the fact that the extensive literature of content analysis offers a number of techniques for dealing with various "psychological" dimensions of rhetorical discourse. As long ago as the 1940s, D. P. Boder was reporting his work with the "adjective-verb quotient"; John Dollard and O. H. Mowrer were describing methods for "measuring tension in written documents"; and R. K. White was developing an elaborate procedure for analyzing psycho-social "values" in message content.[61] In the 1955 symposium on content analysis held at the University of Illinois, George Mahl delivered a paper on "Exploring Emotional States by Content Analysis"; Charles Osgood dealt at some length with contingency and evaluative-assertion methods for arriving at inferences about the message-sender's attitudes; and John Garraty addressed himself to "The Application of Content Analysis to Biography and History." [62]

Since this essay cannot attempt to offer a technological handbook instructing the prospective researcher in the operational details of content analysis, it is not possible to discuss the numerous procedural problems which confront the analyst. Let it simply be said that the rhetorical critic must be prepared to make difficult decisions concerning such matters as the degree to which his analysis is based upon "lexical" (or "sign-vehicle") *versus* "semantic" coding; the determination of "recording units" and "context units"; the generation of categories (topical, thematic, directional), and many others. He will find himself confronted with tough philosophical questions, such as the extent (if any) to which he may infer, from content analysis data alone, the intended "meanings" of the communicator. Content analysis may generate data upon which (especially when combined with other kinds of data) the researcher may attempt to differentiate (1) what the speaker actually said, (2) what the speaker communicated unintentionally, and (3) what the speaker wanted to say. The whole issue of identifying various levels of "meaning" is obviously one which penetrates to the very heart of the rationale of content analysis; it is one on which a variety of conflicting views will be found in the literature.

The position taken here, although supported by many writers in the field, is not to be understood as any kind of unanimous or "official" view. It is simply this: content analysis (of any kind) is a procedure for describing, in various ways, the lexical and/or semantic content of a selected message-stimulus. *In conjunction with other kinds of data,* the output of content analysis may be used as evidence for supporting an almost infinite variety of conclusions about the "stylistic" or linguistic characteristics of the discourse, the supposed goals of the speaker, the personality of the speaker, the speaker's impact upon his audience, the sociopolitical-cultural milieu of the speech, and so on. Taken by themselves— without supplementary support from other kinds of research —the results of content analysis can be used, literally, only as what they really are: ways of describing communication content. In other words, content analysis deals directly with what a communicator actually emits—not with what he intends to say, or wishes he had said, or with what a specified audience thinks he said. This view is obviously congruent with what Osgood and others have called the "representational"—as contrasted to the "instrumental" or manipulative—functions of language.[63] For this reason, content analysis data typically furnish materials supplementary to more ultimate questions than the simple one, "what did the speaker say?" Such data are commonly employed to define in precise terms, for example, the exact nature of the communicative stimulus in experimental studies. (It is interesting to note that Alexander George's well-known successes in "predicting" Nazi intentions during World War II, based upon his so-called propaganda analysis of German mass media statements, actually relied heavily upon a large body of supporting information from a wide variety of noncontent sources.) [64]

It is appropriate, then, to take cognizance here of the most basic—and, in an ultimate or metaphysical sense, perhaps the most insoluble—problem in content analysis methodology: the problem of determining what "meanings" the message-text "really" represents. The same issue can be couched in ontological terms: exactly where does "content" exist? Does it exist in the mind of the original message sender, or in the minds of the various message receivers, or somehow in the lexical words themselves, or in some strange mixture of these? As semanticists have been proclaiming for years, meanings are obviously behavioral phenomena, which we can attribute to human beings (in the present context) and certainly not to marks on paper or sounds in the air. Paraphrasing Irving Lee, people mean, but words in themselves do not. Hence, the locus of speech "content" must lie, ultimately, in the nervous system of *any* human being who receives the communicative stimuli—including, of course, the message sender himself, and unintended as well as intended audiences. In the last analysis, the coder decides in his own mind what meanings to assign the physical signals he is examining, although he should base such critical decisions upon a wealth of supplementary data. Furthermore, he must be scrupulous in specifying *whose* "meanings" (besides his own) he is discussing in a given context. The implication of this line of reasoning would appear to be quite clear: content, except in the trivial sense of physical markings or sound waves, does not possess a single definitive existence; hence, if we were to be properly precise, we should label content analysis something like "a report of what Scholar X believes to be the specified relevant, and most probable, 'meanings' represented by the specified sample of physical records of a selected communication event." [65]

However, this thorny problem has not prevented content analysts from pursuing their trade, any more than it has discouraged literary critics. There are reasonable—although not entirely satisfactory—ways of handling the problem of specifying meaning in content analysis. The textbooks, the manuals, and the published research in the field will supply the interested reader with an explication of these strategies. It will be sufficient here merely to assert that the analyst can utilize various kinds of externally derived evidence, including his own personal familiarity with the symbolic code and perhaps the frame of reference in which the speech is uttered, and he can engage the services of other analysts or coders for purposes of computing rather precise reliability indices. However, there is no denying that certain kinds of discourse are particularly recalcitrant for the content analyst; for example, that which is characterized by highly subtle irony (especially if spoken in an age or in a culture far removed from that of the analyst), by *double-entendre,* by "private codes," or by purposeful ambiguity.

Regardless of the difficulties, the position adopted here is probably best epitomized in the terms suggested by Robert Merton and his colleagues: that the essential office to be performed by content analysis is a comprehensive and systematic "specification of the [communicative] stimulus." [66] After all, without such specification, scholarly treatment of any speech text—whether for critical or experimental purposes—is likely to remain a rather fuzzy, undefined conception of the central communicative object under study. Especially when the critic or experimenter is concerned with supposed effects of speeches, he "can hardly hope to interpret the effects of the stimulus pattern unless the stimulus pattern itself is adequately known." For example, he "may discover that the 'Kate Smith bond appeals effectually led to bond pledges,' without materially adding to our understanding of the workings of persuasion." [67] Such a state of affairs has been compared to the discovery that " 'living in the tropics is a cause of higher rates of malaria'; it is true but unspecific." [68] But even if the critic is more concerned with appraising the "quality" of speaking, rather than with its effects, he can still profit by the use of whatever precision tools he can find for assisting him in apprehending the total critical object, or for ferreting out ways in which the speaker has handled his available means of persuasion. Content analysis procedures offer such precision tools.

There is no blinking the fact that content analysis is far from being a perfect research instrument. It suffers from a number of inherent disabilities. There are unsolved problems of category construction, validity, reliability, and semantics. But any rhetorical critic engages perforce in *some* kind of analysis of speech "content." The central issue is probably this: "Since the rhetorical researcher *must* analyze in some fashion anyway, why should he not utilize the best available tools?" For many rhetorical critics, content analysis will be only one of a variety of techniques (although studies devoted exclusively to analysis per se can certainly be justified). But even as a secondary source of information, content analysis has apparently been employed in only a handful of the hundreds of rhetorical dissertations issued from American collegiate speech departments since the 1920s.

Indeed, some may find it embarrassing to discover that, beginning with the early work of Lasswell and his colleagues in 1940–1941, content analysis—even when applied to the study of speeches and their audience effects—has been developed and employed as a rhetorical tool, not by professional "rhetoricians" but by specialists in such fields as journalism, political science, and social psychology. (It may be especially embarrassing to recall that Merton, a social scientist, in his famous study of the Kate Smith war bond appeals, prefaced many of his chapters with quotations from such sources as Plato's *Gorgias* and Aristotle's *Rhetoric*,[69] or to note that Lasswell explicity characterized content analysis as an extension of rhetorical concepts found in Aristotle.) [70] On the more cheerful side, it is true that in 1962 *Western Speech* published a group of articles under the heading "Symposium on Value Theory and Rhetoric," in which content analysis findings were featured as valuable components of both critical and experimental studies.[71]

Let there be no misunderstanding. Content analysis is offered as no panacea; nor is it proposed as a replacement for historical (or other extrinsic) adjuncts to rhetorical criticism. Rather, content analysis should be regarded simply as a device—albeit an extremely useful one—for assisting the critic in his efforts to come to grips with the central object of his endeavors, the speech itself. There can be no quarrel with Berelson's admonition that "Content analysis can describe communications, but it cannot, per se, evaluate them." [72]

The burden of this paper has been that rhetorical critics can profitably reexamine the premises upon which, following Wichelns, we have abandoned the "literary criticism of oratory." The argument here is not that we should revert to belletristic studies, but that such a reexamination will help us to see more clearly what really happened: while properly rejecting aesthetic *criteria,* we at the same time tended to accept the basic *methodology* of literary scholarship. And this methodology, at least until fairly recently, has been characterized by an extrinsic-historical orientation; hence, it was easy for rhetorical critics to devote more and more of their energies to historical data, while overlooking opportunities to develop techniques for close textual analysis. If we reflect upon the rationale of the New Critics in literary scholarship, it is not for the purpose of imitating their methods or their frame of reference, but rather for finding the inspiration to exploit the potentialities of our own subject matter. Even when we must deal with defective, fragmented, or missing speech texts, we will still find the principles of content analysis applicable to whatever reports are extant. More important than merely borrowing the existing formulations of content analysis, rhetorical critics can exercise their creative faculties to fashion new techniques uniquely designed to deal with the "content" of rhetorical discourse.

If we hold, with Ernest Wrage, that the "basic ingredient of a speech is its content," [73] then we should be uncomfortable in the knowledge that nonrhetorical specialists have done most of the spade work in the content analysis of speeches. This paper began with a warning to literary critics from a literary critic who was disturbed by the spectacle of scholars moving out of their own subject. In words strikingly similar, Wayland Parrish has voiced his fear that rhetorical critics may get "lost in a blind alley" if we stray too far from "the central core of our discipline," [74] and, more recently, Ehninger has warned that traditional criticism may encourage the critic's eye "to wander away from the speech to fix on the environment which surrounds it," and that even when "ideally practiced it does indeed remove the critic from the critical act." [75] Without necessarily committing himself to these views, the rhetorical critic can at least make more of an effort than he has in the past to explore the possibilities of intrinsic criticism.

NOTES

1. Norman Foerster, "The Study of Letters," in *Literary Scholarship*, Norman Foerster, ed. (Chapel Hill: University of North Carolina Press, 1941), p. 217. See also pp. 3–25.
2. Herbert A. Wichelns, "The Literary Criticism of Oratory," in *Studies in Rhetoric and Public Speaking in Honor of James A. Winans*, A. M. Drummond, ed. (New York: Century, 1925), pp. 181–216.
3. S. Judson Crandell, "Good Critical Writing," The Forum, *Quarterly Journal of Speech*, XXXV (December 1949), 511. See also the report of the Committee on Case Studies in American Public Address: "New Directions in Public Address Research," The Forum, *Quarterly Journal of Speech*, XXXV (October 1949), 357–360.
4. Howard Gilkinson, *Outlines of Research in General Speech* (Minneapolis: Burgess, 1943), p. 14.
5. A. Craig Baird, "Opportunities for Research in State and Sectional Public Speaking," *Quarterly Journal of Speech*, XXIX (October 1943), 304–308.
6. Forest L. Whan, "The Speech Profession Jilts Radio," *Quarterly Journal of Speech*, XXX (December 1944), 440.
7. Bower Aly, "The History of American Public Address as a Research Field," *Quarterly Journal of Speech*, XXIX (October 1943), 312.
8. Wayne N. Thompson, "Contemporary Public Address as a Research Area," *Quarterly Journal of Speech*, XXXIII (October 1947), 277.
9. Hoyt Hudson, "The Field of Rhetoric," *Quarterly Journal of Speech Education*, IX (April 1923), 167–180.
10. Wichelns, *op. cit.*, p. 209. It may be noted in passing that this familiar view seems to imply that the speaker-audience relationship is one in which the speaker is engaged in a one-way communication attempt. For provocative recent discussions of the difficulties inherent in such a position, see especially: Raymond A. Bauer, "The Obstinate Audience," *American Psychologist*, XIX (May 1964), 319–328; and Lawrence W. Rosenfield, "Rhetorical Criticism and an Aristotelian Notion of Process," *Speech Monographs*, XXXIII (March 1966), 1–16.
11. See: Loren D. Reid, "The Perils of Rhetorical Criticism," *Quarterly Journal of Speech*, XXX (December 1944), 417; and Lester

Thonssen and A. Craig Baird, *Speech Criticism* (New York: Ronald Press, 1948), p. 327.

12. Wichelns, *op. cit.,* p. 199.

13. *Ibid.,* p. 215.

14. William Norwood Brigance, "Whither Research?" *Quarterly Journal of Speech,* XIX (November 1933), 556.

15. Donald C. Bryant, "Aspects of the Rhetorical Tradition—II. Emotion, Style, and Literary Association," *Quarterly Journal of Speech,* XXXVI (October 1950), 326–332.

16. Donald C. Bryant, "Rhetoric: Its Functions and Its Scope," *Quarterly Journal of Speech,* XXXIX (December 1953), 422.

17. Donald C. Bryant, "Some Problems of Scope and Method in Rhetorical Scholarship," *Quarterly Journal of Speech,* XXIII (April 1937), 182.

18. René Wellek and Austin Warren, *Theory of Literature* (New York: Harcourt, Brace, 1949), p. 4.

19. John H. Randall, Jr. and George Haines, IV, "Controlling Assumptions in the Practice of American Historians," in *Theory and Practice in Historical Study,* Merle Curti *et al.,* eds. (New York: Social Science Research Council, 1946), p. 25.

20. Wellek and Warren, *op. cit.,* p. 7. For useful discussions of the nineteenth-century insistence upon "scientific" history, see, for example: Susanne K. Langer, *Philosophy in a New Key* (New York: Penguin Books, 1948), pp. 225 *et passim;* and Hajo Halborn, "The Science of History," in *The Interpretation of History,* Joseph R. Strayer, ed. (New York: Peter Smith, 1950), pp. 59–83.

21. René Wellek, "Literary History," in *Literary Scholarship, op. cit.,* p. 100; see his entire paper, pp. 91–130; also: Stanley Edgar Hyman, *The Armed Vision* (New York: Knopf, 1948), pp. 11–13; and Harry Levin, "Literature as an Institution," in *Criticism: The Foundations of Modern Literary Judgment,* Mark Schorer *et al.,* eds. (New York: Harcourt, Brace, 1948), pp. 546–553.

22. George Detmold, "Advice to One Entering the Profession—from One Leaving It," *Bulletin of the American Association of University Professors,* XXXVII (Summer 1951), 368.

23. Wayne Shumaker, *Elements of Critical Theory* (Berkeley: University of California Press, 1952), p. 39.

24. *Ibid.*

25. *Ibid.,* pp. 63 and 57.

26. Wellek and Warren, *op. cit.,* p. 139f.

27. Shumaker, *op. cit.,* pp. 50f and 58.

28. William Elton, *A Guide to the New Criticism* (Chicago: The Modern Poetry Association, 1951), p. 4.

29. John Lee Jellicorse, review of Edwin Black, *Rhetorical Criticism* (1965), "New Books in Review," *Quarterly Journal of Speech,* LI (October 1965), 340. (He continues, "Now they are attempting to escape that 'hell of no intentions' by returning to a theory which recognizes that communication is designed for response. . . .")

30. See: Loren D. Reid, "The Perils of Rhetorical Criticism," *Quarterly Journal of Speech,* XXX (December 1944), 415–422; Wayland Maxfield Parrish, "The Study of Speeches," in *American Speeches,* W. M. Parrish and Marie Hochmuth, eds. (New York: Longmans, Green, 1954), pp. 1–20; Albert J. Croft, "The Functions of Rhetorical Criticism," *Quarterly Journal of Speech,* XLII (October 1956), 283–291; Marie Hochmuth Nichols, *Rhetoric and Criticism* (Baton Rouge: Louisiana State University Press, 1963); Edwin Black, *Rhetorical Criticism: A Study in Method* (New York: Macmillan, 1965); and Douglas Ehninger, "Rhetoric and the Critic," *Western Speech,* XXIX (Fall 1965), 227–231.

31. Probably the most comprehensive and definitive statement of this position is that of Thonssen and Baird, *op. cit.;* see especially Chapters 1 and 17, for example the following passages: pp. 5, 9–13, 16–18, 21–23, and 448–450.

32. Ehninger, *op. cit.,* p. 230.

33. For a synopsis of the opposing positions and a closely reasoned support of criticism anchored upon "effect" (a position questioned by the present author), see Thomas R. Nilsen, "Criticism and Social Consequences," *Quarterly Journal of Speech,* XLII (April 1956), 173–178.

34. A. Craig Baird and Lester Thonssen, "Methodology in the Criticism of Public Address," *Quarterly Journal of Speech,* XXXIII (April 1947), 137.

35. Bryant, "Some Problems of Scope and Method," *op. cit.,* p. 184.

36. Dallas C. Dickey, "Southern Oratory: A Field for Research," *Quarterly Journal of Speech,* XXXIII (December 1947), 459. The same writer also has urged that rhetorical critics must "be more than amateur historians." See his article, "What Directions Should Future Research in American Public Address Take?" *Quarterly Journal of Speech,* XXIX (October 1943), 304.

37. Thonssen and Baird, *Speech Criticism, op, cit.,* p. 11.

38. A remarkably explicit statement of the reasoning here suggested may be found in Bryant's article, "Some Problems of Scope and Method"; rhetorical criticism, he argued, "gains its value from its *primary* concern with considerations of audience-speaker-occasion —of background, surroundings, contemporary effectiveness";

hence, analyses of speech content "must remain only exercises" until there is available "rather complete knowledge of the setting" (p. 11; italics added).

39. Shumaker, *op. cit.*, p. 19.
40. *Ibid.*, p. 29.
41. Croft, *op. cit.*, p. 290.
42. Shumaker, *op. cit.*, pp. 35–37.
43. Reid, *op. cit.*, p. 417f.
44. Bernard Berelson, *Content Analysis in Communication Research* (New York: The Free Press, 1952), p. 9.
45. *Ibid.*, p. 17. Pool, viewing the total development of content analysis from a historical perspective, characterized Berelson's book as "the standard codification of the field"; see Ithiel de Sola Pool, "Introduction," in *Trends in Content Analysis*, I. de Sola Pool, ed. (Urbana: University of Illinois Press, 1959), p. 1.
46. Norman John Powell, *Anatomy of Public Opinion* (New York: Prentice-Hall, 1951), p. 96.
47. George A. Miller, *Language and Communication* (New York: McGraw-Hill, 1951), p. 95.
48. Irving L. Janis, "The Problem of Validating Content Analysis," in H. D. Lasswell, Nathan Leites, and Associates, *Language of Politics* (New York: George W. Stewart, 1949), p. 55.
49. See: Leo Lowenthal and Norbert Guterman, *Prophets of Deceit* (New York: Harper, 1949); and Alexander George, *Propaganda Analysis: A Study of Inferences Made from Nazi Propaganda in World War II* (Evanston: Row, Peterson, 1959). Cf. also Ralph Lord Roy's treatment of "Protestant fringe groups promoting hate and disruption" in his *Apostles of Discord* (Boston: Beacon Press, 1953).
50. Ithiel de Sola Pool, ed., *Trends in Content Analysis* (Urbana: University of Illinois Press, 1959); Robert C. North *et al.*, *Content Analysis: A Handbook with Applications for the Study of International Crisis* (Evanston: Northwestern University Press, 1963).
51. Berelson, *op. cit.*, p. 198.
52. Pool, *op. cit.*, "Introduction," p. 2. See also, by the same author, the concluding chapter in *Trends in Content Analysis*, "Trends in Content Analysis Today: A Summary," pp. 189–233.
53. Berelson, *op. cit.*, pp. 121 and 128.
54. James A. Robinson, "Editor's Foreword," in North *et al.*, *Content Analysis, op. cit.*, p. vii.
55. Pool, "Trends in Content Analysis Today," *op. cit.*, p. 196.
56. See, for example, Charles E. Osgood, "The Representational Model and Relevant Research Methods," in *Trends in Content*

Analysis, Pool, ed., *op. cit.,* pp. 54–78; and, in the same volume, Pool, "Trends in Content Analysis Today," pp. 196–202.

57. The original and definitive source is C. E. Osgood, Sol Saporta, and Jim C. Nunnally, "Evaluative Assertion Analysis," *Litera,* III (1956), 47–102. Excellent briefer expositions are to be found in Osgood, "The Representational Model and Relevant Research Methods," pp. 41–54; and in Chapter VI of North *et al., Content Analysis* (pp. 91–102). An insightful critique is included in Pool, "Trends in Content Analysis Today: A Summary," pp. 218–223, who points out that when Osgood and his colleagues devised the techniques of evaluative assertion analysis, they were attacking the problem of validity in the measurement of "valence" in texts.

58. The books by Berelson, Pool, and North, when combined, contain an impressive compilation of the numerous techniques available. It may be important to warn the reader, therefore, that the repertory of content analysis available to the rhetorical scholar includes far more than the "two operations" described by Bormann in his very brief summary, "First, the careful definition of the unit to be counted, and, second, a set of categories used to tabulate the counts." Ernest G. Bormann, *Theory and Research in the Communicative Arts* (New York: Holt, Rinehart and Winston, 1965), p. 377.

59. Nichols, *Rhetoric and Criticism, op. cit.,* pp. 73, 106–107.

60. Black, *Rhetorical Criticism, op. cit.,* p. 24 (italics added). See Martin Maloney, "Clarence Darrow," in *A History and Criticism of American Public Address,* Marie K. Hochmuth, ed. (New York: Longmans, Green, 1955), III, pp. 262–312.

61. See: D. P. Boder, "The Adjective-Verb Quotient: A Contribution to the Psychology of Language," *Psychological Record,* III (1940), 309–343; John Dollard and O. H. Mowrer, "A Method of Measuring Tension in Written Documents," *Journal of Abnormal and Social Psychology,* XLII (1947), 1–32; and three articles by Ralph K. White: "A Quantitative Analysis of Hitler's Speeches," *Psychological Bulletin,* XXXIX (1942), 486–487; "Black Boy— A Value Analysis," *Journal of Abnormal and Social Psychology,* XLII (1947), 440–461; and "Hitler, Roosevelt and the Nature of War Propaganda," *Journal of Abnormal and Social Psychology,* XLIV (1949), 157–174. A detailed exposition of R. K. White's methodology is contained in his monograph, *Value-Analysis—The Nature and Use of the Method,* a publication of the Society for the Psychological Study of Social Issues (Glen Gardner, N. Y.: Libertarian Press, 1951).

62. See, respectively, Chapters 3, 2, and 6, in Pool, ed., *Trends in Content Analysis, op. cit.*

63. See Osgood's chapter, "The Representational Model and Relevant Research Methods" in Pool, ed., *Trends in Content Analysis, op. cit.,* pp. 33–88. Also, in Pool's discussion in his summary chapter (pp. 218–223). For a closely reasoned statement dealing with the advantages of using the "instrumental model" for inferring "emotional states from language behavior" (with the aid of nonlexical evidence), see Mahl's chapter in the same book, "Exploring Emotional States by Content Analysis," pp. 89–130.

64. See Alexander George, "Quantitative and Qualitative Approaches to Content Analysis," in Pool, ed., *Trends in Content Analysis, op. cit.,* pp. 7–32; also his book: *Propaganda Analysis, op. cit.* Note also Berelson, *op. cit.,* pp. 83–90.

65. Cf. Lee O. Thayer, "On Theory-Building in Communication: Some Conceptual Problems," *Journal of Communication,* XIII (December 1963), 217–235. Thayer warns, for example, against reifying a "message" apart from its human sender or receiver, and from its context; and he considers such distinctions as manifest versus latent as "false dichotomies" (pp. 230–232).

66. Robert K. Merton, Marjorie Fiske, and Patricia L. Kendall, *The Focused Interview* (New York: The Free Press, 1956), p. 6; Robert K. Merton, *Mass Persuasion: The Social Psychology of a War Bond Drive* (New York: Harper, 1946), p. 12.

67. Merton, *Mass Persuasion, loc. cit.*

68. Merton, Fiske, and Kendall, *The Focused Interview, loc. cit.*

69. See Merton, *Mass Persuasion, op. cit.,* especially pp. 20, 44, 70, 109.

70. Harold D. Lasswell, "The Language of Power," in *Language of Politics, op. cit.,* pp. 3f., 382–388.

71. See the "Symposium: Value Theory and Rhetoric," appearing in two installments in successive issues of *Western Speech,* under the editorial supervision of Edward D. Steele, XXVI (Spring, Summer 1962), 70–91, 133–145. The articles are: Edward D. Steele, "Social Values, the Enthymeme, and Speech Criticism," pp. 70–75; Theodore Balgooyen, "A Study of Conflicting Values: American Plains Indians *vs.* the U. S. Commissioners of Indian Affairs," pp. 76–83; Edward D. Steele and W. Charles Redding, "The American Value System: Premises for Persuasion," pp. 83–91; Stanley F. Paulson, "Social Values and Experimental Research in Speech," pp. 133–139; Milton Dobkin, "Social Values and Public Address: Some Implications for Pedagogy," pp. 140–145.

72. Berelson, *op. cit.,* p. 46.

73. Ernest J. Wrage, "Public Address: A Study in Social and Intellectual History," *Quarterly Journal of Speech,* XXXIII (December 1947), 454.

74. Parrish, "The Study of Speeches," *op. cit.*, p. 20.
75. Ehninger, *op. cit.*, p. 230.

The Pre-Scientific
Function of Rhetorical Criticism

JOHN WAITE BOWERS

Professor Bowers takes the view that "the rhetorical critic's principal task is to produce testable hypotheses which, when verified, will have the status of scientific laws." In this essay the author discusses the procedures the rhetorical critic must follow if he is to aid in the formulation of such hypotheses and considers opportunities for cooperation between the critic and the scientist in contributing to communications research.

John Waite Bowers is Associate Professor of Speech at the State University of Iowa. His article is printed here for the first time.

Metacritics have attempted frequently to classify rhetorical critics and their functions by establishing a conceptual ideal for criticism and providing embryonic evidence of its fruitfulness. Edwin Black, for example, offers not one ideal but three. Taken together, they will serve as a starting point for this essay.

The author's first definition of the function of a critic comes at the beginning of a comparison between critics and scientists:

Both the critic and the scientist have in common two vitally important activities, which are to see a thing clearly and to record what they have seen precisely. Beyond these activities, which might serve as a greatly simplified characterization of the means of science, we need add only one other item to complete the snapshot of the critic: he also seeks to judge the thing justly.[1]

At this point, we are told that the critic has three duties: accurate perception, accurate reporting, and just evaluation. The first two are identical with the duties of a scientist; the last is beyond science.

Fourteen pages later, Black seems to have changed his mind about the functions of the critic, for he says, "Criticism has no relationship with its subject other than to account for how that subject works; it demands nothing but full disclosure." [2] The critic seems now to have become exactly equivalent to the scientist, for "full disclosure" presumably results from accurate perception and accurate reporting. Criticism, apparently, need not "judge the thing justly."

Finally, Black adopts a third frame of reference in his attempt to demonstrate the inadequacy of a popular critical system. Citing Theodore M. Greene, he uses a chapter to illustrate three "constituents" of criticism: the historical, the recreative, and the judicial.[3] Again, the critic must evaluate as well as explain.

All three of the definitions assume that the critic, rhetorical or otherwise, concerns himself primarily (and possibly exclusively) with the explication and evaluation of a single piece of work in a single context. This essay will take the point of view that rhetorical criticism has a much nobler end: to contribute to an economical set of scientifically verifiable statements accounting for the origins and effects of *all* rhetorical discourses in *all* contexts.[4] This point of view requires that rhetorical criticism be viewed as an early part of a process eventuating in scientific theory. Hence, the adjective "pre-scientific" is appropriate.[5] The term implies that, in this frame of reference, the rhetorical critic's principal task is to produce testable hypotheses which, when verified, will have the status of scientific laws. It ignores, though it does not prohibit, the critic's evaluative activities.

The rest of this essay will amplify the methods, requirements, and potential of the pre-scientific use of rhetorical criticism. Like other metacritical essays, it will include embryonic evidence supporting the fruitfulness (and, implicitly, the
shortcomings) of the approach advocated. The amplification
requires three sections: (1) an exposition of the scientific
method, (2) a description of the requirements imposed on
the pre-scientific critic by the method, and (3) an analysis of
problems in communication theory where the pre-scientific
critic could make immediate contributions.

I

Science is the search for relationships between antecedents
and consequents.[6] It attempts to explain (that is, enable predictions about) things and events in terms of other things and
events. Another way of expressing the same thought is to say
that science searches for functional relationships.

Typically, this search follows certain well-defined steps.
First, the scientist discovers, somehow, a hypothesis he wants
to test. This hypothesis is a hunch, a guess about functional
relationships. It is a tentative generalization which totters
feebly on the foundation of common-sense observation. All
of Aristotle's descriptive statements are of this type. The scientist admits that his hypothesis is based on only a few infor-
mally observed instances. He frankly concedes that the relationships he observes may be coincidental rather than
functional. I will call this first hypothesis-forming stage of
science the pre-scientific stage. Most rhetorical critics and
"theorists" [7] in the past have operated at this stage whenever
they have asserted relationships between the speaker's personality and speech behavior, or between speech behavior
and its effects, or among these three elements. I consider this
pre-scientific stage to be the part of the scientific process
where the rhetorical critic could perform a most useful function; hence, the real burden of this essay is to suggest ways

that rhetorical critics could enhance their value as formulators of hypotheses.

The scientist's hypothesis must meet certain requirements if it is to be helpful in the later stages of the scientific process. It must be phrased and amplified in such a way that any other scientist, given reasonable intelligence and comparable equipment, can test the same hypothesis. Often, although not necessarily, the scientist expresses the variables in his tentatively asserted functional relationship as quantities. Certainly, if he asserts that more or less of something is functionally related to more or less of something else, he must specify how one can reliably recognize "more" and "less." Even if he simply asserts a presence and absence relationship between two variables, he often finds numbers useful. Whether or not he uses numbers, the scientist must define his variables *operationally;* that is, he must in effect say to others: if you perform such-and-such action or series of actions with so-and-so things, what you observe will be what I mean when I use the term variable X.

Once the scientist has defined operationally the crucial terms in his hypothesis, he proceeds to test it. His test of the hypothesis may take many forms, and for a fair test he need not employ all the statistical paraphernalia currently popular. Frequently, that paraphernalia is useful to give assurance that his results could not easily be accounted for by chance. He need not even use the experimental method, although that method helps to insure that he is observing functional relationships rather than more of the coincidences upon which his hypothesis might have been based in the first place. What he *must* do as a test of his hypothesis is to make predictions from it, predictions which should be confirmed in some situation where the antecedent variable is at work. The situation must be replicable; that is, he must test his hypothesis in such a way that other scientists can test the same hypothesis in a comparable way.

If the scientist confirms his hypothesis, he is in a position to formulate it as a *law,* a statement of fact relating the antecedent to its consequent. This law may express a strong functional relationship or a weak one; that is, the scientist may predict from the law exact or gross results on the consequent from variations in the antecedent. Frequently, because of the many unknowns operating in his studies, the scientist in communication research must express his laws in statistical, as opposed to individual, terms; his laws lack the rigor necessary for predictions about individual behavior.

If he fails to confirm his hypothesis, the scientist is slightly better off than he was before, for he has acquired from his failure additional information which should enable him to formulate an improved new hypothesis as well as to devise more efficient ways of testing it. He is likely to speculate from his results that the operation of the variable he was manipulating was overshadowed by the power of another, uncontrolled variable. Hence, we often see in the literature *post hoc* explanations of unexpected results from scientific studies in public address. We should not accept these generalizations as though they were scientific laws, for they are not. They are, rather, only slightly-improved (because of more information) versions of the pre-scientific hypotheses of the rhetorical critic.

But suppose that the scientist confirms his hypothesis, thereby raising its status to that of a law. He publishes his law as well as an account (operational definitions and all) of the evidence upon which it is based. Presumably, he is not working in isolation. Other scientists interested in the same general area of research are formulating and testing other hypotheses, which, when confirmed, become other laws. At some stage this more-or-less unsystematic proliferation of laws should make incarnate a theorist, the messiah of science. The theorist uses precisely the same methods as his more mundane brother, but he uses these methods on nobler material. Instead of relating things or events to other things or events, he relates scientific laws to other scientific laws. Hence, his statements are much more powerful—permitting predictions in a much wider range—than are the laws of his predecessors. Frequently, he uses constructs (for example, "force" in physics, "drive" in psychology), variables which are not directly observable, in his theoretical statements. Nevertheless, like the ordinary scientist, the theorist must use terms which are operationally defined and which refer eventually to things and events which can be reliably, if indirectly observed by anyone with the appropriate tools. Also like the ordinary scientist, the theorist must make statements in such a way that they will generate predictions (new hypotheses) which, if confirmed, would disprove the theory; that is, the theory must have built into it clearly defined predictions which could lead to its own destruction or alteration.

In short, science proceeds from hunches about functional relationships (first hypotheses), the statements which the rhetorical critic is uniquely qualified to formulate and which I have called pre-scientific, to tests of the predictions made by those hypotheses. Those tests will produce laws, or, at least, systematic observations which lead to new hypotheses (second hypotheses). The synthesis of laws gives birth to theory, statements relating laws, which in turn generate predictions of a still higher order (third hypotheses). The entire process is characterized by the precision of its definitions and the open nature of its methods. Given the proper tools, anyone with evidence can dispute or qualify any scientist's statements on his own grounds, using scientific methods. Hence, many people call science a self-correcting process.

Perceptive critics will have noticed by now that the distant goal of science in rhetoric is to establish generalizations governing the art of which Plato had Socrates speak in the *Phaedrus:*

> Since it is in fact the function of speech to influence souls, a man who is going to be a speaker must know how many types of souls there are. Let us, then, state that they are of this or that number and of this or that sort, so that individuals also will be of this or that type. Again, the distinctions that apply

here apply as well in the case of speeches: they are of this or that number in type, and each type is of one particular sort. So men of a special sort under the influence of speeches of a particular kind are readily persuaded to take action of a definite sort because of the qualitative correlation that obtains between speech and soul; while men of a different sort are hard to persuade because, in their case, this qualitative correlation does not obtain.[8]

Plato probably wrote the passage to demonstrate the impossibility of an exact art of rhetoric. Scientists in communication, however, are audacious enough to aspire to the complete knowledge of which Plato writes. With the cooperation of rhetorical critics, their aspirations could be less unrealistic.

II

What does science, aiming at theory, require of the pre-scientific critic? That is, if the rhetorical critic wants to aid in formulating hypotheses, what requirements must he meet?

Clearly, he must learn the habit of defining his terms operationally. He must learn to specify the variables with which he is concerned in such a way that others may recognize and manipulate those same variables. Discriminating though his own sensibilities may be, the critic must translate his perceptions into statements and directions which his scientific colleague can understand. This task is more difficult than he might think. An example will clarify the nature of the defining requirement.

In 1960, "language intensity" became an experimental variable in communication research. Needless to say, the notion of intensity, or emotionalism, had been a popular one in rhetorical criticism. A few experimental studies using related concepts had been executed, but intensity remained operationally undefined.

One definition, offered by content analyst Bernard Berelson, follows:

> Intensity: This category, sometimes called "emotionalism" or "sentimentalization" . . . refers to the "strength" or "excitement value" . . . with which the communication is made. In many cases the analyst is interested in gauging the relative intensity of different contents, particularly because this factor is believed to be especially effective in influencing readers and listeners. Thus the "emotional component" of communication content is a relatively popular category for analysis.[9]

The definition obviously offers no operational terms. "Strength" and "excitement value" are more vague even than "intensity."

Jack Matthews, in an early communication research effort, had experimentally manipulated "loaded language."[10] In his study, however, he had defined "loaded language" by writing the same newscast in three versions: a strongly pro version, a neutral version, and a strongly anti version. Although he then exposed these versions to the independent judgment of others, his method would be difficult to repeat on other messages, especially if the new study required some assurance that no content variables were being confounded with the language variable.

The operational definition of language intensity required an elaborate system, which is described in detail elsewhere.[11] The method required samples of people from the experimental population to be used as judges of intensity. Since terms which are intense to one individual may not be intense to another, the mean judgment of a group of raters was used as the index of intensity. After having intensity defined as "the quality of language which indicates the degree to which the speaker's attitude toward a concept deviates from neutrality," the raters assessed it as they viewed alternative words and phrases in the context of a persuasive communication. Therefore, the mean rating of the group of raters became the operationally-defined intensity of any given word or phrase. The mean rating of all the manipulated words and phrases in any given form of the communication became the operationally-defined intensity of that form of the communication. The method met the supreme test of an operational definition. Wendel Thompson was able to manipulate intensity in later persuasive communications using exactly the same procedure.[12]

Achieving success in operationally defining a critical term so that it can be employed in communication research is a relatively trivial matter. It is worth mentioning only because it illustrates the potential of rhetorical critics for contributing to the scientific study of communication. The task of defining intensity would have been much easier if a perceptive critic had defined it earlier in a way permitting reliable redefinition with manipulation of the variable as the aim. Conceivably, the critic might even have used numbers to index levels and classifications of intense language as he perceived them.

Besides developing a skill in operationally defining the variables he perceives, the contemporary rhetorical critic who wishes to function prescientifically must acquire knowledge of the results of communication research studies relevant to his criticism. This knowledge will enhance the value of his criticism in two ways: (1) it will prompt him to arrive at conclusions (hypotheses) which have not already been responsibly tested, thereby producing more useful predictions; and (2) it will enable him to "predict backwards," thereby furnishing further tests of the communication research results relevant to his own studies.

The research on language intensity, for example, revealed that the variable was correlated with a number of other variables.[13] The highest correlation was between intensity and metaphorical quality, a relationship which was perfect (1.00) for what were called sex metaphors and death metaphors in the experimental messages. That is, audiences consistently perceived certain kinds of metaphors as more intense than any literal equivalent.

Other experiments, however, showed that under certain conditions highly intense persuasive messages which contained metaphorical as well as literal evaluative terms had less effect on attitude change than did less intense messages.[14] This discovery, together with the correlational findings, led to speculation that in certain persuasive situations metaphors, especially sex and death metaphors, would have boomerang effects. That is, experimental results led to the prediction that some kinds of persuasive speeches containing abundant evaluative expressions couched in metaphors would bring about less attitude change in the advocated direction than would their less intense, more literal equivalents.

A colleague whose main interest is in rhetorical criticism, Michael Osborn, strongly disputed the negative conclusion about the effects of metaphor. In support, he cited such "theorists" as Aristotle, Quintilian, and Cicero, and such practitioners as Demosthenes, William Pitt, Abraham Lincoln, William Jennings Bryan, and Franklin Delano Roosevelt. Without further empirical evidence, obviously the dispute would have remained unresolved.

Therefore, this interaction between scientific and critical knowledge prompted an experiment to test the effects of metaphors in persuasive speeches.[15] A relatively straightforward resolution of the disagreement would result from the testing of the two demonstrably intense types of metaphors, sex and death, against their literal equivalents. Since the practice of noteworthy speakers had been to use metaphors most liberally in the conclusions of speeches, the experimenters included them only in the last two paragraphs. Hence, the experiment tested the effects of a speech concluding in a "sex" metaphor against its literal equivalent and a speech concluding in a "death" metaphor against its literal equivalent. If the metaphorical speeches had less effect than their literal counterparts, the disputants could agree that metaphor, like other intense language, had a boomerang effect. If on the other hand, the metaphorical speeches were more successful, at least two explanations would be possible: (1) the effects of metaphor differ from the effects of other kinds of highly intense language, or (2) metaphor and possibly other kinds of highly intense language enhance attitude change when confined to the conclusion of persuasive speeches.

The study showed unequivocally that the speeches with metaphorical conclusions brought about more attitude change in the direction advocated than did speeches with literal conclusions. (The possible explanations for this finding remain to be tested.) An interesting secondary finding was that the two kinds of metaphor differed in their effects on judgments of the credibility of the speakers.

The metaphor study illustrates the considerable value derived from the pooling of critical and scientific resources. Without Osborn's knowledge of rhetorical criticism, an experiment on the effects of metaphor probably would have taken a different form. Without the empirical research skills available, Osborn probably would not have experimented with the effects of metaphor at all. The experiment contributed insights into both criticism and communication research. Osborn has since received a research fellowship to study intensively, "predicting backwards," the use of metaphor by speakers in the eighteenth century. In short, the study is evidence of the desirability of knowledgeable interaction between the rhetorical critic and the student of communication research. It confirmed a critical hunch and forced the alteration of a scientific statement which was approaching the status of a law. Its results must be taken into account in future communication research and can be projected in rhetorical criticism to the past, though at considerable risk.

III

The potential of informed and sophisticated rhetorical critics for pre-scientific contributions to communication research should be obvious. Assuming that such critics exist or will exist, what should be their particular concerns if they are to be immediately valuable?

Adopting the frame of reference proposed here may be

especially difficult for many critics accustomed to considering form and content in speeches as inseparable, for experimental methods permit the heuristic separation of variables even though those variables may always be combined on the platform. If he is to make a pre-scientific contribution, the rhetorical critic must (though, perhaps, grudgingly) also separate variables, even though he may perceive that eventually he will recombine them for a "complete" criticism. Hence, this discussion will consider content and form separately while recognizing that they merge in real life and in the most sophisticated scientific laws. In other words, the discussion will first treat the problem of content, then the problem of form, and finally the problem of form/content interaction. Obviously, this treatment ignores many relevant variables outside the message, including all extrinsic ethical variables. Certainly, these extra-message variables are appropriate subject matter for communication research, but, for the purposes of this paper, explicit consideration of them would be premature. Sooner or later, communication science will contain laws about extremely complex interactions, but this discussion will concern itself only with the message.

The problem of content. "Content" means here a message's assertions about things, persons, and events and about the relationships among things, persons, and events in the observable world outside the speaker. Content variables include evidence or supporting material, and "logic." Consider, for example, the following passage from a speech used in several experiments:

In 1959, American women squandered 27.4 billion dollars on the gruesome clothes which the fashion industry produces. This gigantic figure represents more than a quadrupling of the amount spent by the same group of women in 1935. Of the 27.4 billion dollars, gullible teenagers spent 3.2 billion—half the amount spent by all women in 1935—while their more antique sisters spent 24.2 billion.

If we had the impulse, we could easily express the content of the passage algebraically. For example, each expression below represents one sentence in the passage. Where W equals the amount women spent on clothes produced by the fashion industry in 1959, X equals the amount spent in 1935, Y equals the amount spent by teenagers in 1959, and Z equals the amount spent by all other women in 1959:

$W = 27.4$ billion
$W = 4X$
$W = 27.4$ billion $= (Y = 3.2$ billion $= .5X) + (Z = 24.2$ billion$)$

While the content of all messages cannot be expressed algebraically so simply, the exercise illustrates the definition of "content." By examining the algebraic expressions, we immediately perceive a number of content variables which could be treated separately or together. For example, we might choose to vary simply the size of the numbers in the passage to find out how that variation affects audiences. Or, noting that the third statement is highly redundant, we might delete some terms and/or add others. We might add entirely new content elements, for example, attributing the figures in the passage to a source thereby adding to the definition of each algebraic term. We might even introduce some erroneous logic, asserting, for example, that Z equals 9.5 billion when, according to the other information given, it must equal 24.2 billion. Any of these operations would change the content of the message.

The problem of form. "Form" means here any message variable not included in the definition of "content." These variables include the choice and arrangement of words and their delivery which give cues to the attitudinal or mental state of the source of the message. We are interested, of course, in the effects these variables might have on the attitudinal and mental states of audiences.

In the passage just cited, for example, the speaker chose some words implying an extreme attitudinal state toward some content elements. The word "squandered" tells us not only that women spent money but also that the speaker strongly disapproves of their spending. "Gruesome" reflects the speaker's strong disapproval of the appearance of the clothes upon which women spent the money. "Gigantic," "gullible," and "more antique" all are cues to negative attitudes. These words give clear evidence about the speaker's evaluation of things, persons, and events and their relationships rather than about the realities themselves. Other, less dramatic expressions in the passage also give us information about the speaker. He says, for example, "represents more than a quadrupling of the amount" when "is more than four time as large as" would have been equivalent in content. We might infer from this choice the speaker's assessment of his audience, and we might measure the effects of the two versions on a given kind of audience.

Like the choice of words, their arrangement may alter the effects of a message without altering its content. More difficult to define operationally and to manipulate are delivery variables, paralanguage and kinesics, which are important in and unique to oral communication.[16]

The problem of form/content interactions. Although communication research may profit most immediately from further studies in the separate effects of form and content variables, the problems of greatest interest to the critic are those involving form/content interactions. Suppose, for example, that the passage about women's fashions cited earlier had been found (as it has been) to change attitudes in the direction advocated less effectively than a less intense passage with equivalent content. A naïve interpretation of this finding would be the generalization: highly intense language has a boomerang effect.

As was noted earlier, however, one study demonstrated

the opposite effect when highly intense language was metaphorical and when it was confined to the conclusions of
speeches. In other words, the evidence indicates that language
intensity interacts with other formal variables in such a way
that its effect on attitude change cannot be expressed in a
simple antecedent-consequent generalization. The generalization must contain some "ifs" and "excepts."

Undoubtedly, our knowledge of relationships between
speeches and their effects will become more complex when
we begin to consider the interactions among form and content
variables. If, instead of "women's fashion changes," the topic
of the highly intense speech were "the Japanese government,"
and if (to introduce another kind of variable) the speech had
been delivered in late 1941, and if (to introduce still another
kind of variable) it had been delivered by Franklin Delano
Roosevelt, would we expect intensity to boomerang? Obviously, we would not. But what are the elements, the variables,
that make us say "obviously"? How can we define them operationally and test them experimentally? If the rhetorical critic
will direct himself at answering these two questions, he can be
extremely valuable to the development of theories of communication.

IV

This essay has argued that the interaction between critics and
scientists in communication could be more productive if critics would take as one of their primary activities the formulation of testable hypotheses. It has defined at some length the
methods leading to and the values realizable from such a systematic relationship. In short, it had advocated for rhetorical
criticism and communication research more pattern and less
serendipity. Would the outcome be worth the effort?

Some critics would answer negatively. They would base
their reply on two statements: (1) generalizations derived

from criticism require no further confirmation, and (2) even if critical generalizations did require further confirmation, communication research would be no help, for it only establishes the obvious.

Black amplifies the first objection:

> We shall not assume it necessary to pile up a quantity of empirical evidence to establish a generalization. The logic of criticism is not always a logic of probabilities; the recurrence of a phenomenon does not necessarily strengthen a critical generalization. Criticism's rationality, rather, may sometimes resemble the logic of the chemist. Once the chemist has combined two parts hydrogen to one part oxygen to produce water, his formulary generalization is secure. For the chain of events to have occurred once is sufficient to establish it as a potentiality forever. Similarly, when the critic abstracts a formula from a single phenomenon of discourse, that single occurrence is enough to establish the formula.[17]

The answer to the objection is a relatively easy one. If a chemist observed *in nature, without controls,* that two parts hydrogen and one part oxygen formed water, and if he then promulgated his generalization *without attempting to duplicate the phenomenon in the laboratory,* he would cast grave doubts upon his scientific competence. His colleagues probably would not accept the generalization (though, in this instance, it is a valid one), for it would not have been properly verified.

The critic observes *in nature, without controls.* Although any one of his generalizations might be valid, he has no assurance that all of them are not based on coincidence. To increase his confidence in the validity of the antecedent-consequent relationships he asserts, the critic must employ something approaching experimental methods. He must make it impossible for uncontrolled, unperceived variables to operate systematically. He must make successful predictions in controlled situations. To paraphrase a colleague: The critic thinks he knows; the scientist knows he knows. If our aim is rigorous theory, we must establish firm low-order laws by more than informal observation and highly inferential statements based on that observation.

The second objection, that communication research only establishes the obvious, is more difficult to answer. A noteworthy rhetorical critic gave it articulate expression in the final Ph.D. examination for a candidate who had attempted to measure the differential effects of certain kinds of communications on frustrated and ego-satisfied subjects.[18] The candidate had found, not surprisingly, that frustrated subjects responded much more negatively to certain concepts related to their frustration than did ego-satisfied subjects.

In a way, the candidate was discovering the obvious. Probably, very few studies in communication research will have surprising results, for human communication behavior has been subject to direct and conscious scrutiny by a great number of intelligent people. Their speculative, pre-scientific hypotheses probably do not contain many glaring inaccuracies. Without glaring inaccuracies, no possibility exists of dramatically disproving traditionally held beliefs about communication. We cannot expect any scientific debunkers to match Galileo, Harvey, and Newton.

But the candidate did more than the examiner was willing at that moment to give him credit for. For one thing, he made the obvious more precise than it had been previously. He was able to express quantitatively the effects on the reception of a communication of the psychological conditions he tested. For another thing, he was able to show that the frustrating manipulation was much more effective as an agent of attitude change than was a persuasive communication designed to change attitude in the same direction. Finally, he had accumulated his evidence in such a way that his findings can be directly and with great confidence applied to future research in communication and in rhetorical criticism.

We must recognize that the two kinds of scholars, experimentalists and critics, are not in competition, even though they may find each other mutually unintelligible at times. By their attempts at affecting each other, they may either facilitate or impede progress toward communication theory.

NOTES

1. Edwin Black, *Rhetorical Criticism* (New York: Macmillan, 1965), p. 4.
2. *Ibid.*, p. 18.
3. *Ibid.*, p. 36.
4. Black understands this function of criticism, though he does not include it in his definitions. In Chapter V, "An Alternative Frame of Reference," he outlines some basis for speculation about the relationships among "rhetorical strategies, rhetorical situations, and audience effects" (pp. 132–137).
5. This essay owes much to Albert J. Croft, "The Functions of Rhetorical Criticism," *Quarterly Journal of Speech,* XLII (October 1956), 283–291; and Martin Maloney, "Some New Directions in Rhetorical Criticism," *Central States Speech Journal,* IV (March 1953), 1–5. I have taken the term "pre-scientific" from Maloney.
6. For representative sources of the following, see: Gustav Bergmann, *Philosophy of Science* (Madison: University of Wisconsin Press, 1958); and Herbert Feigl, "Naturalism *and* Humanism," *American Quarterly,* I (1949), 139–142.
7. I enclose theorist in quotation marks because, as will become apparent later, I reserve the term for another kind of person.
8. Plato, *Phaedrus,* trans. W. C. Helmbold and W. G. Rabinowitz (New York: Bobbs-Merrill, 1956), p. 63.
9. Bernard Berelson, *Content Analysis in Communication Research* (Glencoe, Ill.: The Free Press, 1952), p. 160.
10. Jack Matthews, "The Effect of Loaded Language on Audience Comprehension of Speeches," *Speech Monographs,* XIV (1947), 176–186.
11. John Waite Bowers, "Language Intensity, Social Introversion, and Attitude Change," *Speech Monographs,* XXX (November 1963), 345–352.
12. Wendel Lawrence Thompson, "Message Intensity as a Variable in the Application of the Congruity Principle and Message Discrepancy Theory," unpublished Ph.D. dissertation (University of Iowa, 1956).
13. John Waite Bowers, "Some Correlates of Language Intensity," *Quarterly Journal of Speech,* L (December 1964), 415–420.
14. Bowers, "Language Intensity, Social Introversion, and Attitude Change," *op. cit.*
15. John Waite Bowers and Michael M. Osborn, "Attitudinal Effects of Selected Types of Concluding Metaphors in Persuasive

Speeches," paper presented at Speech Association of America convention, New York (December 1965).

16. For one attempt, see John Waite Bowers, "The Influence of Delivery on Attitudes toward Concepts and Speakers," *Speech Monographs*, XXXII (June 1965), 154–158.

17. Black, *op. cit.*, p. 137.

18. The candidate was Carl William Carmichael, "Attitude Change as a Function of the Relevance of Communications and Their Sources to Frustrating Experiences," unpublished dissertation (University of Iowa, 1965). The examinar was Donald C. Bryant. Since the position attributed to Bryant here was expressed as a series of questions in an examination, it does not necessarily represent his point of view.

Toward a Pluralistic Rhetorical Criticism

MARK S. KLYN

The dissatisfaction with much that passes as theory and prac-
tice of criticism is sharply revealed in Professor Klyn's essay.
He cites the preoccupation with pedagogy as the main cause of
the narrowness of view—the emphasis on effect—that has
characterized rhetorical critics. He finds that even those who
have ostensibly broken with the Aristotelian tradition have not
been able to free themselves of its limitations. "Rhetorical
criticism," Klyn concludes, "delimits only a genre, an area of
concentration . . . it does not define a methodology. Rhetor-
ical criticism . . . should only mean intelligent writing about
rhetoric."

Mark S. Klyn is Assistant Professor of Speech at the Uni-
versity of Washington. His article is printed here for the first
time.

I

In this essay I want to make a case that is rooted in conclusions which seem almost self-evident to me, but that, as
far as I know, is only now being advanced in the literature of
rhetorical criticism. My contentiousness is purposed, thus, to
join in yet another round in that rebellion against the oppression of the conventional, very limited, rather sterile—but
"academically respectable"—attitude which still dominates

our conception of rhetorical criticism. Wearing though it is, this "war of liberation" must go on until it is won.

The position for which I wish to argue is, in essence, that "literary criticism" and "rhetorical criticism" should be taken as truly parallel, and thus that the term "rhetorical criticism" delimits only a genre, an area of concentration; that it does *not* define a methodology, as rhetorical critics seem conventionally to have supposed.

Rhetorical criticism, I think, only means "intelligent writing about works of rhetoric"—or about works which are not "rhetoric" in any formal sense but which can be illuminatingly treated from such a standpoint—in whatever way the critic can manage it. It does not imply a prescriptive mode of writing, any categorical structure of judgment, or even any judgmental necessity.

II

This stance, I suppose, remains generally unorthodox. The demand for a prescriptive rhetorical criticism, built on a standard methodology, sacrificing ingenuity for dependability, has been "normal" in the field. L. H. Mouat, for instance, once put it this way: "It is not the purpose of this essay to make a brief for a *particular* set of principles that will bind rhetorical concepts, but rather to urge that there be a *single* set of principles." [1]

Professor Mouat expresses a desire for unity which is typical of rhetorical critics, but it seems delusive to me—as ephemeral as his distinction between "making a brief" and "urging." (How can one "urge that there be a *single* set of principles," without at least implying what one "particularly" thinks they should be?) This monistic compulsion in the theory of rhetorical critics points to a decisive misapprehension about the nature of criticism and what one should ask of it.

Those who demand of rhetorical criticism that it be founded upon some unifying set of principles seem to me not to be talking about "criticism" at all, but about pedagogy. Their penchant to blur the distinction between these two disciplines has been both the burden and the curse of rhetorical critics; they have purchased the teacher's authority at the cost of the critic's freedom.

This blurring, this ambiguity at the heart of things—and the insecurity which has often caused it, as well as the ambivalence it has often sponsored—has indeed been pervasive in rhetorical criticism, and has generated the monism against which I am arguing. Perhaps rhetorical critics have gained some measure of stability from their absolutism, but it has been a false security built upon an arbitrary limitation of the critic's function and a confusion of his role.

III

A more recent example of this problem seems evident in a new book on rhetorical criticism by Anthony Hillbruner.[2] Professor Hillbruner sometimes talks as though he envisions an eclectic rhetorical criticism freed from the strictures enforced by a rigid tradition, as in these passages:

> That there is no one critical approach to speaker, speech, and audience has now been accepted. Art is long. It has manifold ramifications.[3]

> The art of public address, encompassing both social and rhetorical factors, is as complicated as life itself because it studies a medium of communication which concerns itself with every meaningful facet of life, and if public address is complex, it follows that its criticism will also be.[4]

But Hillbruner seems to shy away from the full effect of this standpoint, and his relativism is often more apparent than real. When he does come to specify concretely just what rhetorical critics should *do,* Hillbruner sometimes seems as committed to the notion that there exists an ideal, totalistic pattern of rhetorical criticism as his predecessors, despite his questioning of their insularity and narrowness. His is a wider ranging, more elastic formulation than the conventional view, but it still seems absolutistic at the core:

> The general aim of the critic of public address is to discover what happened as a result of a given speech or a series of speeches. Specifically, such a study can take two distinct routes. The first is to determine the immediate effects of the speech. The second is to discover what the long range effects were.[5]
>
> The aim of this search is to discover the factual and functional relationships among the speaker, the audience and the occasion. . . .
>
> Moreover, the use of these extrinsic components with their psychological and sociological overtones, is still only prelude. It is a prelude to the discovery and understanding of what the speaker actually did, from the standpoint of content and form, in adapting his message to the hearers within their immediate environment.[6]

Thus, despite Hillbruner's awareness of the limitations of conventional rhetorical criticism and the breadth of his critical concerns, he still seems inhibited by the monism which has been traditional in his discipline and continues to envision rhetorical criticism as a unitary pattern of analysis and evaluation. (Only the pattern, for him, has become so broad and multifarious, so all-inclusive, that to accomplish a critical appraisal, the rhetorical critic could only be some sort of vast universal mind grandly cognizant of *everything*—in a word, of "life itself.")

IV

I would argue, on the contrary, that it is not at all patently necessary for the rhetorical critic to discover "what the speaker actually did" or "what happened" as a result. It is essential for the *teacher* of rhetoric to do so to be sure; but why is it necessary for the critic?

No paradox is intended. If the critic can find out, for example, something of what a rhetorical work has *meant* (which may be unrelated to what was intended, or to what was done, even to "what happened" in any concrete sense), surely this is, *in itself,* a very useful critical activity—even though it may teach a would-be speaker nothing about the practice of his art.

Clearly, in the traditional *modus operandi* of rhetorical criticism, the critic has been imagined primarily as a teacher, concerned less with the illumination of particular works of rhetoric, of speakers, or of movements than with putting his insights to use practically, as generalizations, so that he might teach others to speak well. At least, this seems the implicit premise which has governed the effort of our critics of rhetoric, supporting an attitude of functionalism which is quite false to the nature of criticism.

This pedagogic compulsion which has dominated rhetorical criticism—making it, in this sense, "sophistic" rather than disinterested—is, again, rooted in a misconception—not of the function of rhetoric but of the nature of criticism. For the *practice* of rhetoric, the emphasis seems quite sound, and it has proved eminently workable. But for the *criticism* of rhetoric, it has generated a severely limiting set of priorities, the limits growing out of the assumption that the job of the critic is essentially to be useful to the practitioner. And this, it must follow, he could only be by producing "technical" criticism concerned basically with the intricacies of rhetorical strategies and the "effects" they are thought to have produced.

The bias toward pedagogy has thus manifested itself concretely as a "technical" absolute for rhetorical criticism. This attitude seems to me quixotic at best, censorious at worst. Its weakness would be obvious if one were to say, in a parallel sense, "The task of the critic of fiction is to teach his readers to write their own stories," or "The task of the movie critic is to teach his readers to make their own films."

True, a focus on the technical is the bent of *one* sort of criticism, but only of *one*. For the critic, speaking in general terms, can one say more than that his task is to be intelligent and perceptive, and to be "useful" to anyone who would better understand—practitioner, detached observer, or what have you?

V

The traditional pedagogical fixation of the rhetorical critic is rooted, as are most absolutes in this field, in his understanding of Aristotle's *Rhetoric*. Edwin Black has called this bias toward the technical, in its contemporary form, "neo-Aristotelianism." [7]

This standpoint successfully avoids the restrictiveness which would make rhetorical criticism hopelessly partial if it were to proceed within the limits established for literary criticism. Clearly, the abstractness inherent in literary criticism's necessary *text*-centeredness would not be appropriate for a work of rhetoric, which is far too "worldly" and interconnected with its society to be realistically considered a self-contained "aesthetic object."

But paradoxically, rhetorical critics, in a parody of Aristotelian rigor, have substituted their own arbitrary limitations for the austerity of literary criticism. These are strictures of technical pragmatism confining the critic to the immediate, audience-oriented situation of the speech, or at least to the practical argumentative ends of the rhetoric—to find, in Hillbruner's words, how the speaker has "adapt [ed] his message to the hearers within their immediate environment."

I do not think that this sort of insularity is reasonable— or even necessarily "true to Aristotle." The *Rhetoric* is a practical treatise—a "textbook" people would say now—clearly designed for instructional uses. Its technical concerns are dictated by its very practical ends. But there is no *necessary* reason to think that it must also be regarded as definitive for rhetorical criticism. As Black has written, "Aristotle could define the scope and technique of the deliberative orator, but he did not write on the scope and technique of the critic of deliberative oratory." [8]

The problem with the traditional view of rhetorical criticism is not inherent in the Aristotelian conception of rhetoric, but obtrudes only when this standpoint is extended to dominate rhetorical criticism as well. Not that practice and criticism are unrelated—only that their relationship is not inevitable or, from the critic's standpoint, even "necessary."

Many men have been very effective persuaders while knowing nothing (or at least seeming to practice nothing) of rhetorical theory. With neither diffidence nor self-consciousness, we should admit the converse: that rhetorical criticism can be valuable regardless of its consideration of the practicalities of rhetorical theory. Otherwise, for the rhetorical critic, we only authorize a tyranny of technique.

VI

The most important result of the monistic attitude is that conventional rhetorical critics have tended to delimit the meaning and consequence of a work of rhetoric in a special, very narrow way. This, in turn, has led them to erect the deceptive and confining standard of "effect" as the ultimate test of critical judgment.

The Aristotelian standpoint toward the practice of rhetoric is founded in its identification of a rhetorical deed as a very concrete, purposeful act, which has its *raison d'être* in the results that it is able to achieve in its immediate situation —especially in terms of the response of its actual audience. On this basis, Aristotle differentiates between "rhetoric" and "poetic," holding that the former is a useful art, functional in intent and pragmatic in process, while the latter is a fine art, purposive only in its design to create a thing of formal beauty, and timeless and universal in its consequences.

Working from this formulation, Herbert A. Wichelns, in his germinal essay "The Literary Criticism of Oratory," sharpens the definition to distinguish rhetorical and literary criticism.[9] In so doing, he emphasizes the functional immediacy of rhetorical practice to the point where it also becomes a coercive necessity for rhetorical criticism. The attitude that Professor Wichelns approves is found, for example, in the "suggestions of a new point of view" in E. P. Whipple's essay on Webster, about which Wichelns writes:

> It is the point of view of the actual audience. To Whipple, at times at least, Webster was not a writer, but a speaker; the critic tries to imagine the man, and also his hearers; he thinks of the speech as a communication to a certain body of auditors. . . . What is significant in Whipple's essay is the occasional indication of a point of view that includes the audience.[10]

Later in his essay, Wichelns makes categorically explicit the pragmatic, technical bent of his conception of rhetorical criticism. In what are probably the most influential few lines in modern American rhetorical criticism, he writes:

> If now we turn to rhetorical criticism . . . we find that its point of view is patently single. It is not concerned with permanence, nor yet with beauty. It is concerned with effect. It regards a speech as a communication to a specific audience, and holds its business to be the analysis and appreciation of the orator's method of imparting his ideas to his hearers.[11]

Wichelns does go on to speak of the rhetorical critic's inevitable concern with the ideas and values of a people as they are influenced by a leader who necessarily "belongs to social and political history." [12] But in the pragmatic, technical scheme in which they are placed, such intimations of a broader critical scope can have little weight as priorities.

VII

Professor Wichelns' essay, in 1925, was a great liberating, even iconoclastic statement, giving substance and structure to a study which heretofore had been formless and ephemeral. Thus, its great and lasting effect: it literally *created* the modern discipline of rhetorical criticism. If its doctrine has become something of a "sacred cow," it is largely the fault of the timidity and conformity of succeeding generations of rhetorical critics. But it is also true that Wichelns' essay does lend itself to this sort of institutionalization; in its very strength is an implicit absolutism.

"The Literary Criticism of Oratory," in the way it extends the precepts of the *Rhetoric* concerning rhetorical practice, aggrandizing them into final standards for rhetorical criticism, prepares the way for the very limited, monistic theory of rhetorical criticism advocated by later critics. The theory is expounded, for example, by Lester Thonssen and A. Craig Baird in their *Speech Criticism,* perhaps the most authoritative of modern treatises in this field.[13] Thonssen and Baird are forthrightly absolutistic in erecting Wichelns' test of a speech's "effect" on its immediate audience and how this result is thought to have been achieved, as the ultimate concern of rhetorical criticism:

> . . . most basic is the critic's evaluation of the speaker's ability to adjust his argument to the four factors of rhetoric as developed by the ancients: himself, his audience, his subject, and the occasion. Of these, most important is the audience, for the success of a speech lies not in its well-turned phrases, but in its achieving a desired effect upon its hearers. Thus the primary concept is that of speech as communication, i.e., the

degree to which it achieves an end consistent with the speaker's intention.[14]

With similar certitude, William Norwood Brigance, prefacing the first two volumes of the *History and Criticism of American Public Address,* writes:

> That public address may have permanence and aesthetic excellence is not denied, nor is it ignored; but final judgment is here based on effect instead of beauty, on influence instead of appeal to the imagination.[15]

In this development from Wichelns to the more contemporary critics, one can see the transformation of a legitimate Aristotelian concern into an oppressive and insular critical orthodoxy stressing the pedagogical absolute of "effect." As Black puts it, "There is little disposition among neo-Aristotelian critics to comprehend the discourse in a larger context. . . . To the neo-Aristotelian, the discourse is discrete and its relevant effects are immediate." [16]

By this transformation, the practical has become the mundane, the technical, the arid. For rhetorical criticism, the narrowness and sterility of the product of this transformation has been palpable; the *irrelevance* of our work is proof enough.

VIII

Surely many people working in this field have wondered at the fact that the best "rhetorical criticism" we have had—the most intelligent, perceptive writing about persuaders or works of rhetoric—has come from writers unaffiliated with the academic discipline of speech. I mean criticism such as Kenneth Burke's essay on Hitler, Edmund Wilson's on Lincoln, Perry Miller's on Jonathan Edwards, Harry V. Jaffa's study of the

Lincoln-Douglas Debates, or almost all of Richard Hofstadter's writing, but especially the essays collected in *The American Political Tradition* and *The Paranoid Style in American Politics.*[17]

The field of speech has produced nothing to compare with such criticism. Indeed, the title "rhetorical critic," and the attitude which has usually accompanied it, seem almost to have constituted a positive disability, unsuiting the writer for work of the highest quality and intelligence.

Why? I think that the most important reason for his weakness has been the rhetorical critic's domination by the monistic, pedagogically oriented theory of criticism which has disabled him, inhibiting and constraining his critical intelligence. The only factor joining the diverse historians and literary critics I have singled out is that, in writing about persuaders or works of rhetoric, they have functioned as *free* men, unfettered by any coercive critical doctrine, unconfined by any pedagogical imperative, able to reason inductively from their material and to explore their insights as independent, disinterested thinkers. This freedom, I believe, is a *sine qua non* for the true critic.

The traditional view of rhetorical criticism, then, cuts all the wrong way. It tries to establish a prescriptive definition of rhetorical criticism, rather than being content with a generic identification, which would leave the critic uninhibited methodologically and free to use his mind as well—perhaps, as unconventionally—as he can.

That this monism has been essentially thoughtful and well-intentioned is indisputable. But it has resulted in a kind of tyranny, nonetheless. Again, it is not the status of this theory as *one* viable critical approach that I would question, it is only the tyranny of its monism with which I would contend.

NOTES

1. L. H. Mouat, "An Approach to Rhetorical Criticism," in *The Rhetorical Idiom,* Donald C. Bryant, ed. (Ithaca: Cornell University Press, 1958), p. 165.
2. Anthony Hillbruner, *Critical Dimensions: The Art of Public Address Criticism* (New York: Random House, 1966).
3. *Ibid.,* p. 5.
4. *Ibid.,* p. 159.
5. *Ibid.,* p. 59.
6. *Ibid.,* p. 32.
7. Edwin Black, *Rhetorical Criticism: A Study in Method* (New York: Macmillan, 1965), pp. 27–35.
8. *Ibid.,* p. 3.
9. Herbert A. Wichelns, "The Literary Criticism of Oratory," in *Studies in Rhetoric and Public Speaking In Honor of James Albert Winans,* A. M. Drummond, ed. (New York: Century, 1925), pp. 181–216. Reprinted in *The Rhetorical Idiom, op. cit.,* pp. 5–42.
10. Wichelns, *op. cit.,* p. 198.
11. *Ibid.,* p. 209.
12. *Ibid.,* p. 215.
13. Lester Thonssen and A. Craig Baird, *Speech Criticism* (New York: Ronald Press, 1948).
14. *Ibid.,* p. vi.
15. William Norwood Brigance, "Preface," in *A History and Criticism of American Public Address,* I, William Norwood Brigance, ed. (New York: McGraw-Hill, 1943), p. viii.
16. Black, *op. cit.,* p. 33.
17. Kenneth Burke, "The Rhetoric of Hitler's 'Battle'," in *The Philosophy of Literary Form,* rev. ed. (New York: Vintage Books, 1957), pp. 164–189; Edmund Wilson, "Abraham Lincoln: The Union as Religious Mysticism," in *Eight Essays* (New York: Anchor Books, 1954), pp. 181–202; Perry Miller, "The Rhetoric of Sensation," in *Errand into the Wilderness* (New York: Harper Torchbooks, 1964), pp. 167–183; Harry V. Jaffa, *Crisis of the House Divided* (New York: Doubleday, 1959); Richard Hofstadter, *The American Political Tradition* (New York: Vintage Books, 1954); Richard Hofstadter, *The Paranoid Style in American Politics and Other Essays* (New York: Knopf, 1965).

On the Varieties
of Rhetorical Criticism

OTIS M. WALTER

Professor Walter sees rhetorical criticism as a liberal art, and a much neglected art in view of the need for intelligent assessment of speaking, which is so important to our public and private lives. Traditional criticism, in Walter's view, has been much too narrowly conceived, based as it has been on a limited interpretation of Aristotle's Rhetoric. *Each act of criticism, he argues, should be a unique act, beholden to no tradition but that of intellectual integrity. We are asked to analyze and evaluate the* act of communication *in human affairs—rhetoric is extended to include the* talk *of men throughout virtually the entire spectrum of social interaction.*

Otis M. Walter is Professor of Speech at the University of Pittsburgh. His article is printed here for the first time.

I

Speaking, so commonplace in every culture, now and then becomes a powerful force affecting individual men and whole civilizations, leading at times to greatness and at times to catastrophe. The speaking of Socrates, made famous by Plato's *Dialogues,* resulted in nothing less than a philosophic revolution; hardly a school of philosophy exists in the Western world that does not find some of its roots in Socratic thought. The speaking of Jesus launched a new religion, and the speaking of the Apostle Paul altered that religion in ways probably unintended by the Founder. Speaking lulled the Romans to disregard the poverty—intellectual as well as economic—of the Roman World until impoverishment produced the sleep that led almost imperceptibly into death; only the final result, the barbarian invasion, was cataclysmic. Speaking intensified the senseless ardor of the Crusades, and later helped to split into a hundred pieces the oldest institution in the Western world. In more recent times, the speaking of Lenin helped create the Russian revolution and lead the Russians into Communism. The speaking of Hitler was indispensable in building the Third Reich, and was an indirect cause of history's most devastating war. Franklin D. Roosevelt, in his first inaugural address, restored, by a single speech, the confidence of Americans in their economic future. Throughout the country, almost universal despair gave way to hope as he announced, "The only thing we have to fear is fear itself." Winston Churchill, despite the disaster of Dunkirk, steeled the British Empire to the seemingly impossible task of achieving victory.

In the past, wherever social, political, economic, religious, and philosophic revolutions have arisen, speaking has played an important role—sometimes desirable and sometimes disastrous. Today, the power of speeches is even greater than in the past, for now a speech can be heard and the speaker seen around the world as the words are spoken.

Speeches, of course, embody ideas—thoughts and feelings given life by the total personality that delivers them. All of the ideas that affect us, however, do not come to us through speeches; the written word in its many forms is, in fact, our greatest source of ideas. But the spoken word, active and vibrant, has an impact that written passages rarely, if ever, can match. There are, of course, many influences that shape our behavior: our biological heritage, physical and social environment, the political and economic system we live in, our training, the whole pattern of needs we experience,

intellectual and emotional as well as physical. The speaking
we hear is not separate from other life experiences—it deals
with political and economic issues, social and religious questions, indeed with the whole range of human problems. But
clearly we are shaped in a peculiarly significant way by what
we hear, and are sometimes powerfully moved, as individuals
and as societies.

II

Because speeches are a powerful force, man needs profound
and searching insight into the speeches he hears—into their
truth or falsity, their wisdom or stupidity, their profundity or
emptiness, into their subtle greatness or disguised and hidden
meanness. Since man needs such insights, he needs rhetorical
critics.

In a democratic society, moreover, rhetorical criticism is
especially important. In a democracy, each man must understand and judge what he hears, and therefore each man must
be at times his own rhetorical critic. Unless citizens can judge
wisely what they hear, a free society is virtually impossible.
Since each citizen must distinguish those speeches that should
shape society from those that should not, democracy requires
good rhetorical critics.

To say that democracy requires good rhetorical critics is
to say that rhetorical criticism is a liberal art. A liberal art is
simply an art appropriate to men that are free. ("Liberal"
comes from the Latin, *libero,* to free.) Free men must be able
to accept or reject the speeches they hear, to modify or qualify these speeches, to question them, to doubt them, or to
accept them. Rhetorical criticism, although it has never held
a place among the great liberal arts, deserves one, for it is
appropriate to free men, and, for the fullest exercise of freedom, ever necessary. But despite the need for it, we have little
good rhetorical criticism; of such as we have had, three
sources of it are worth a note. Typically, most rhetorical criti-

cism comes as a by-product of, or as incidental to political, legal, or social "opposition": the party out of power needles the administration in power; the defense attorney exposes the weaknesses in the prosecutor's case; the candidates for office clash—or exhibit their dullness—on television; the leftist lampoons the rightist, and so on. In addition to criticism from opponents, the reaction of the audience (or what psychologists call "feedback") provides a second source of criticism: the audience cheers or "boos" the speaker, or greets him with icy irresponsiveness; the congregation nods in somnolence during the Sunday sermon; the constituents vote their candidate into office. Criticism from opponents and feedback from audiences constitute the main sources of speech criticism today.

Neither of these forms of criticism, nor both of them together, insure that we will have the best, or even adequate, criticism, for both of them are too often tainted. The reactions of opponents and of audiences may spring largely from prejudice; the listeners may be insensitive and ignorant and their reactions inarticulate or haphazard. We need better criticism than that afforded by the unsystematic and uncritical offerings of opponents and audiences.

The trained rhetorical critic constitutes a third source. One would think, if speech criticism is important, that interest in the work of the trained rhetorical critic would be great. But there is no such interest. The world at large takes no note of the work of the professional rhetorical critic. Although the educated part of the world often seeks the work of the dramatic critic, the literary critic, or the art critic, it ignores the rhetorical critic. The very much smaller scholarly part of the world likewise passes by his work. The few who read the works of the rhetorical critic are, themselves, rhetoricians; even they are dissatisfied with current rhetorical criticism, and more than one is bored by it.

If rhetorical criticism is necessary, why are professional rhetorical critics ignored? Many reasons account for the inability of current rhetorical criticism to capture interest, and most of these reasons are beyond our control. One reason, however, is totally within our power to eliminate; this reason, moreover, is a decisive one. Let us look at it.

Most rhetorical critics today use a system derived from Aristotle's *Rhetoric,* a book deservedly listed among the Great Books because it furnishes insights into people, into the process of argument, into the means of persuasion, and into the mechanism of human judgment; it furnishes more of such insights than any similar work. But the *Rhetoric* was not intended as a recipe book for critics; not one line in the *Rhetoric* suggests it was so intended. The results of the use of this otherwise great work as the basis for speech criticism have been largely sterile. But how can so great a book as this be so sterile when adapted to the criticism of speeches? The reason is that the *Rhetoric* is used—or rather, misused—to provide only one aim for criticism, and that aim is not always the most appropriate nor does it provide the most insight. One of Aristotle's stated aims was to ask "what are the means of persuasion?" Adapting this question to criticism, rhetorical critics have asked "to what extent did this speaker use the available means of persuasion?" At one time, forty years ago, this question appeared to be a good one, for it gave the rhetorical critic a sphere of inquiry that seemed exclusively his, one that no literary critic nor dramatic critic had exploited. The exclusiveness of the "Aristotelian" question blinded many to the fact that the question itself was not always worth asking.

Of course, this Aristotelian question often is worthwhile in the classroom where the teacher attempts to impart principles of persuasive speaking. But even in the classroom, the instructor may wisely abandon an analysis of persuasive devices to point out more important matters. If a student, for example, were to use the best available means of persuasion to convince an audience that there were 10,572 beans in a jar he held, few instructors would feel moved to congratulate him. Criticism of such a speech requires no erudite analysis of the persuasive devices used but, rather, a convincing message from the instructor or the listeners that the subject was a waste of the audience's time and a perversion of the speaker's intellect. Aristotle, very likely, would have said as much.

If an analysis of the means of persuasion is not always the best standpoint from which to look at a classroom speech, it is even less satisfactory as a standpoint from which to view historically significant speeches.* Concern only with the means of persuasion often misses important matters. Some examples will illustrate the point. Intelligent men still read Pericles' "Funeral Oration." But the intelligent man—even the intelligent rhetorician—does not ask "how and to what extent did Pericles persuade the fifth-century Greeks who heard him?" We don't know who heard him, and couldn't answer the question if we wanted to. Discerning and sensible men have been asking better questions of this speech for 2,500 years, such as "what, according to Pericles—or was it Aspasis, who may have 'ghosted' the speech—are the characteristics of a free society?" or "How does Pericles' treatment of the free society compare with Milton's in his *Areopagitica* or with John Stuart Mill in his *On Liberty?*" or "Was ancient Athens the kind of society Pericles describes?" These questions have little to do with the available means of persuasion, and yet are better questions than those about the use or neglect of persuasive devices.

Is it, after all, of much importance whether or not the Sermon on the Mount used the available means of persuading the audience of shepherds and fishermen? Suppose we found that the Speaker missed using some means of persuading the Galileans He addressed? Would not one be tempted to say "so what?" It might, indeed, be fascinating to find that the Speaker's means of persuasion were thoroughly consistent —or inconsistent—with His ethical doctrines, yet the most

---

* Even here, however, it is sometimes worthwhile. The aim of Lincoln's "First Inaugural Address" was to prevent the Civil War. It is intriguing to ask "Did Lincoln use all the available means of preventing a civil war?" as did Professor Marie Hochmuth Nichols in *American Speeches* (New York: Longmans, Green and Co., 1954), p. 21–71.

fundamental question would surely be different from the Aristotelian question. More likely it would be "what is the ethical
doctrine expressed in the Sermon on the Mount?" or "what
changes in Old Testament morality did the speaker present?"
Again, neither the most intelligent nor the most fundamental
issues are always revealed by asking about the means of persuasion.

Moreover, total reliance on questions about the means of
persuasion often results not merely in unimportant but sometimes in absurd questions. What is the best way—the most
intelligent way—to view Hitler's anti-Semitic diatribes? Is it
to ask, "Did Hitler use all the available means of persuading
Germans to hate Jews?" And who would assign to Hitler a
lesser degree of significance if we discovered that these diatribes failed to use some way of making men hate, or much
admire him if we found he used all of them? Indeed, we ought
to note the techniques that the demagogue uses, but however
well or ill adapted to the audience these techniques are is
somewhat beside the point. One could better ask "What conditions produce such a speaker and such audiences?" and
"How can such conditions be prevented?" Indeed, the devices
that Hitler used illuminate Hitler and Hitlerism, but the effectiveness or ineffectiveness of the devices is not always the
most critical concern.

The analysis of the "Gettysburg Address" presents nearly
an impossible case for the Aristotelian. He must ask "How
well did Lincoln use the available means of persuasion on his
audience?" But the question can't be answered because we do
not know Lincoln's audience. Most likely, he did not address
the speech to those who stood before him: Lincoln did not
wait for the crowd to be quiet when he gave the speech and
never spoke loudly enough to be heard by more than a small
percentage of those present. The speech was addressed,
rather, to posterity. How well adapted was this speech to posterity? We cannot answer the question for we do not know the
nature of posterity, or even, in these days, whether we will be
fortunate enough to be followed by posterity. Since we do not

know the nature of posterity, we cannot tell if the speech is adapted to it. It is ridiculous to avow that the only proper way of looking at a speech is the Aristotelian way when that way would sometimes leave rhetorical critics with nothing to say!

Thus to ask "Does this speech use the available means of persuasion?" is not always the best question. Although critics were attracted to the question because it offered one that rhetoricians could exploit exclusively, Aristotelian criticism does not meet even the requirement of exclusiveness. Studies of the means of persuasion are not unique to rhetoric: psychologists and sociologists also inquire into the devices of persuasion. Uniqueness, moreover, is hardly a guarantee of excellence. Too much concern with mere uniqueness will relegate rhetorical studies to only those questions about which no one else cares. We should be more concerned with our intellect than with our uniqueness, for uniqueness is easy to come by; intelligence is somewhat more rare, and at the same time more beneficial to humanity.

Regrettably, however, rhetorical critics have made from Aristotle a canon, a creed for criticism. We must not forget that a creed, although it sometimes clarifies and illumines, may become a subtle "enforcer," a guide to the stupid, a tool of the arrogant, and a wall in front of one who realizes that what is intelligent in any given case cannot be dogmatically proclaimed by a code. Instead of guaranteeing good criticism of speeches, the current use of the *Rhetoric* formalizes a way of looking at a speech that is not always the best way, and is sometimes an absurd or impossible way.

III

Rhetorical theory can help free rhetorical criticism from the Aristotelian approach. Although Aristotle defined rhetoric as the art of discovering the available means of persuasion, rhetoric, broadly speaking, is *any theory about communication.*

Theories about communication, from the time of the pre-Socratics to the present, are characterized by great variety; indeed, even many writers on rhetoric have not been predominantly interested in persuasion. These other theorists of communication, who are often neglected in surveys of rhetorical theory, have ideas that can be adapted to rhetorical criticism, and, thereby, can help provide the sense of variety in approach that rhetorical criticism needs. Let us look at some of their theories.

Protagoras presented a series of fragmentary ideas about rhetoric that contrast markedly with the ideas of those who were simply interested in persuasion. He started with the idea that speech should be as intelligent as possible rather than as persuasive as possible. His idea of intelligence was a unique one, and was the ancestor of Hegel's dialectic: when intelligence pushes to its furthest limits, it reveals "two *logoi* in opposition," or two opposites, each of which are true. Protagoras based his theory of rhetoric on the idea that, metaphysically, the world consisted of irrefutable and irreconcilable contradictions. Speech, to be as intelligent as possible, must reveal these contradictions, for they are present in every subject.

A complete rhetoric following Protagoras' idea was never written. If it had been (and I suspect it wasn't written because the product of intelligence, most likely, is not two contradictories), we would have had a description of how to locate, step by step, each of the "two *logoi* in opposition," and how to present each of them so an audience would recognize that they represent intelligence pushed as far as intelligence can go. Even from this brief analysis, we can see that Protagoras was concerned with kindling the intelligence of the speaker and then of the audience; kindling intelligence is different from discovering a way of persuading an audience.

The problem now arises: how can we use "the rhetoric of intelligence" in criticism? Well, first of all we can't immediately, because it hasn't been formulated. No rhetoric attempts to demonstrate how a speaker may push his intellect as far as it can go. Yet one can ask of a speech, "Is this the best that intelligence can do on this subject with this audience?" The question is sometimes a better question than "did this speaker use the available means of persuasion?"

Many other views of rhetoric are available, and most of them are about as undeveloped as that of Protagoras. Yet they contain the unifying *principle* of a possible rhetoric, the *starting point* for further inquiry, the *basis* for a different rhetoric, a *productive assumption* leading to a theory about communication, a *pattern of inquiry* leading to new principles of symbolism, or a different *definition of rhetoric*. What one calls these emphases matters little, but that different emphases exist in rhetorical theory seems utterly beyond dispute. Let us examine some of these differences.

A major objective of both Isocrates and Cicero was to produce the ideal citizen, the orator-statesman. Their interest was not merely in producing those who could persuade, but rather in producing those who would speak in such a way that they would guide an entire culture wisely. Isocrates and Cicero wanted to produce articulate world citizens, identified with more than achieving their own immediate needs, dedicated to the good of the culture as a whole. Their rhetorics, although sometimes more fully formulated than that of Protagoras, were still incomplete, especially that of Isocrates, who does not seem to have written a rhetoric, as such, at all. Cicero's rhetoric, in addition, seems somewhat corrupted by the traditional rhetorical practice of the day so that he is not always devoted to the question "How may speech be taught so as to produce ideal citizens?" but sometimes slips into expediency not entirely compatible with his ideal. Nevertheless, these men represent an interest distinct from one in mere persuasion. The study of their ideal might suggest ways of looking at speeches that might at times be more appropriate than the way of Protagoras or the overused one of Aristotle.

One can return to Aristotle, moreover, and find an emphasis different from the one rhetorical critics have traditionally exploited. One of his more difficult themes is that the rhetorician must have both a deep and broad competence. Rhetoric, for Aristotle, was concerned with politics, and hence, the speaker must use political themes; he must know the subjects of debate at the time and understand the era's problems, possibilities, and dangers. But politics, to Aristotle, was merely *ethics in the large.* The speaker must be master of *ethics* for many lines of argument will be derived from ethical principles, and he who knows the most about them will have the greatest assortment of arguments from which to choose. But the rhetorician must also be a psychologist to judge which arguments appeal to persons in various situations. Thus, to judge a speech one must be a master of politics, ethics, and psychology. Few critics have asked "To what extent does this speaker exemplify the breadth and depth required?" Thus, the present use critics have made of the *Rhetoric* by no means exploits the whole of the work; there are other aspects of it that might furnish more productive questions than the traditional one.

Rhetorical theory furnishes many other suggestions for rhetorical criticism. We might expound on the possibilities of Idealism in Plato's works and in "Longinus." One might find ideas that could be applied to criticism in Quintilian's characteristic educational emphasis, in Augustine's insistence that his religion demanded a characteristic rhetoric, in Bacon's approach to rhetorical logic and to faculty psychology, in the esthetic concerns of Blair, in Campbell's many-sided *Philosophy of Rhetoric,* in Whately's logical emphasis, in Winans' adaptation of the psychology of William James to rhetoric. I. A. Richards attempted to define rhetoric as "a study of misunderstandings and its remedies." And there are other theories of rhetoric as well.

The study of rhetorical theory, therefore, can help inject into rhetorical criticism variety in view and freshness in approach. Once the "cake of custom" is broken, rhetorical theory, provided it is viewed in its diversity, may stimulate the development of ways of looking at a speech that do not yet receive treatment in rhetorical theory. For example, there is no "rhetoric of sanity," but one might ask "What kinds of speaking help lead to serious maladjustment, and what kinds to mental health?" That there are such kinds is suggested by the speaking of Hitler which seemed to convert a whole nation to insanity. Although we need a "rhetoric of sanity," it has not been written, and although we also need to know the ways in which a people may be *led away from* sanity, we have little understanding today of what these ways might be. In addition, communication is one of the links in the chain of causes that leads whole civilizations to develop and grow; there must be kinds of communication that are more civilizing than others and we need to know what these kinds are. We need to understand, likewise, the kinds of rhetoric that may weaken or destroy the civilizing propensities present in a culture.

Indeed, the points of view from which rhetorics might be written seem unlimited. What kinds of rhetoric lead us toward (or away from) the open society? What kinds of rhetoric lead to creativity and to the lack of it? What kinds lead to violence and what kinds to problem solving? What kinds lead to understanding, to high morale, to learning, to dedication, and to their opposites? We need to look at speeches, at times, from all these points of view. There are more worthwhile "undiscovered" rhetorics than there are developed ones, and more ways of looking at a speech critically than even the diverse history of rhetoric suggests.

So far, we have talked about *explicit* rhetorics: consciously formulated theories of communication. Only a few societies have produced such rhetorics, the most notable of which are Greco-Roman civilization and Western civilization. Nevertheless, every culture, and every subculture has an *implicit* theory of rhetoric—a theory of how communication ought to proceed, and of what is appropriate, dangerous, unusual, or saintly. Unexpressed and implicit theories of rhetoric exist in all cultures and subcultures: in aboriginal tribes, in slum culture in our large cities, and "in-groups" and "out-groups." These implicit theories of communication are the distinctive marks that stamp one as a taciturn New Hampshire farmer, as a child of the slums, as a product of university education, as an introvert or an extrovert. Yet we have not uncovered these implicit assumptions about communication, perhaps because we have been too dominated by the study of the available means of persuasion. Nevertheless, we could uncover implicit rhetorics by studies of the communication of any group. Such studies would help reveal the ways in which such groups both communicate and view the communication they hear. Moreover, such studies would provide additional points of view from which a critic might look at a speech.

IV

To assume that rhetorical theory can furnish a formula complete with a step-by-step procedure to be followed by the otherwise thoughtless critic, is likely in error. Formulas may work well in elementary physics, but in the humanities, formulas somehow result in mindless mechanicalness, giving evidence sometimes of hard work but less often of brilliance. Scholarship and hard work are not the same thing; but criticism that is brilliant is always criticism that could *not be easily prescribed,* that is somewhat unexpected, that fits the unique speech for which it is designed and perhaps no other speech, that is the most appropriate thing to say at *this* time about *that* speech. To say that criticism cannot be formulated in advance is only another way of saying that rhetoric belongs to the humanities and not to the natural sciences.

Although humanities at their best do that which is unpredictably and even surprisingly appropriate, the way to such achievement can at least partly be prepared. We must remember, nevertheless, that in the humanities, the perfect idea for criticism springs from the keen intelligence and sensitivity of the critic and not fully grown from a formula out of the past.

In a real sense, *fine* criticism cannot be taught by rhetorical theory or by any other device.

But to say that *fine* criticism cannot be taught is no more than saying one cannot teach great speaking, or brilliant writing, or indeed, virtuosity in any field. Nevertheless, schools can impart a sense of what is worthy, competent, and sensible. If medical schools, for example, cannot automatically produce great surgeons, they still can teach students procedures of good surgery, the problems involved, and the dangers to avoid. Rhetorical theory can serve likewise to point out varieties of criticism that might free the young critic from the notion that there is only *one true way* of criticism; it can suggest to him that there are several ways, some of which are sometimes more appropriate than others. In short, rhetorical theory can suggest to the student that there is not just one or four ways of looking at a speech, but that there are many. The study of rhetorical theory can especially impart flexibility, for rhetorical theory itself is varied; rather than treating only persuasion, some rhetorical theories are not even much concerned with persuading, but with a dozen other matters. Hence, the study of rhetorical theory can help provide the student with divergent standpoints from which he may view speeches, and perhaps help develop the flexibility needed by a good critic. Rhetorical theory can, in addition, give some procedures that might help the critic exploit these standpoints, and give him a sense of the problems and dangers involved in the various ways of criticism. Rhetorical theory cannot be expected to furnish the *perfect way* for the mature scholar, nor will it instruct the unusually brilliant critic, who himself will erect landmarks. Rhetorical theory, like the Emersonian conception of books, should be used "to inspire," although it cannot furnish *one true key* to speech criticism.

Of course, there are other ways to assist the development of good criticism, and these too should be used: one can have the student *practice* criticism of speeches and criticize his practice; one can furnish the student with *examples* of criticism and have him analyze and perhaps emulate the examples; but one function of rhetorical theory can be to give the student some broad *principles* of good criticism and have him try them out. Some combination of the three is probably best.

V

In summary, man needs the best insights possible into speeches. Rhetorical criticism, however, has become formalized by adopting a portion of Aristotle's *Rhetoric;* that portion cannot always provide the insights we need. We need, rather than a single approach to criticism, a great variety of approaches suggested by the explicit rhetorics of the Western world, and that might be suggested by the yet undescribed implicit rhetorics that exist everywhere.

To put it more succinctly, we need a kind of "natural selection" among rhetorical theories. But for natural selection to occur, one must first have *variation,* in the same sense that Darwin recognized in *Origin of Species*. When variations occur, they will compete with the effect that the best adapted at the time will more likely survive. But the starting point must be variation. When we have a number of standpoints from which to criticize speeches, we will be able to select those that most meet our needs.

Selected Writings on the Criticism of Public Address

BARNET BASKERVILLE

In this two part essay—the original Western Speech *article and an addendum—Professor Baskerville surveys the literature on rhetorical criticism, characterizing individual works, noting significant issues, indicating trends and innovations.*

Rather than rewriting the original essay and attempting to interpolate within the appropriate categories items published since 1957, Professor Baskerville has chosen to present the essay essentially as it first appeared and then to add a supplementary statement bringing it up to date. He believes that in this way it is possible to demonstrate more clearly the changed nature of the commentary on criticism during the last ten years. The complete bibliography, including items added at this writing, follows the article.

Barnet Baskerville is Professor of Speech and Chairman of the Department of Speech at the University of Washington.

Attention is frequently called to the substantial body of critical comment upon public speaking which members of our profession have produced in the last quarter of a century. With the publication of the third volume of *A History and Criticism of American Public Address* and in view of the scores of articles and doctoral dissertations on individual speakers and speeches appearing annually, Professor Wichelns' 1925 observation that "We have not much serious criticism of oratory" is no longer applicable. But the period which produced such an abundance of critical literature on speaking has not been characterized by a corresponding interest in discussing the act of criticism itself. We have had prior to the last few years relatively little evaluation of criticism as an art or craft —its methods and standards, its problems and rewards, its philosophical principles. Evidence of paucity of this kind of writing is found in the recent *Index to the Quarterly Journal of Speech,* 1915–1954 prepared by Giles W. Gray. This index lists only three items under *rhetorical criticism* and only about a dozen under *criticism.* The great bulk of entries (25 pages) under *rhetorical criticism* in the *Supplement* to Thonssen and Fatherson's *Bibliography of Speech Education* (1950) are studies of individual orators; only a little over a page is devoted to items on critical methods, and many of these are books on literary criticism. The original *Bibliography* (1939) included no sub-section at all on critical methods.

Moreover, the bibliographical articles which appear annually in our professional journals fail to acknowledge in their subject headings the existence of articles on criticism. Haberman's annual "Bibliography of Rhetoric and Public Address" has no criticism category; items under the general heading *Public Address,* aside from studies of the actual practice of public speaking, are listed either as *History-Culture* or *Theory.* Consequently, such an item as "Emerson As a Critic of Oratory" appears under *Platform Address: Practitioners,* and "Rhetorical Criticism: A Burkeian Method" is classified as *Modern Public Address: Theory.* In Auer's series on doctoral dissertations in progress there is a well-established section on criticism under *Theatre,* but none under *Public Address.* Hence, "An Evaluation of the Criticism of the Oratory of Franklin D. Roosevelt" is listed under *Public Address: Rhetoric.* The same study (an analysis, it will be noted, of the criticism of his speeches, not of the speeches themselves) later appears in Knower's "Graduate Theses" under *Public Address: Orators.*

All this is no reflection upon the bibliographers' ability to classify correctly. Their subject headings are designed to cover, in the fewest possible categories, the items with which they must deal. If sufficient articles, books, and theses appeared annually to warrant a separate category on criticism, it would doubtless be provided—as it has been in some cases under *Theatre*. The fact seems to be that the quantity of such writing has been so small that bibliographers have simply squeezed it into whichever established category seemed least inappropriate.

Since, therefore, articles dealing directly with the methods, standards, and underlying principles of criticism are often difficult to locate and recognize in the available bibliographical sources—since a distinction is seldom made between essays about criticism of speaking and critical essays on speakers—this bibliographical essay is provided as a kind of ready guide to published writings on rhetorical criticism.

Our bibliography will be limited almost exclusively to articles and essays, since we have only one complete volume devoted to instruction in the systematic criticism of speeches. This book is, of course, *Speech Criticism,* by Lester Thonssen and A. Craig Baird, and it is too well known to need much comment here. It is a pioneer work of which our profession is understandably proud. Being a pioneer work, it has had to cover an almost impossibly broad area; it packs into 500 pages an amazing amount of material, including a survey of classical and modern rhetorical theory, a summary of ancient and contemporary criticism, and an extensive discussion of critical standards embodying and supplementing the classical divisions of rhetoric. It provides, therefore, in certain areas at least, little more than suggestive outlines for further more limited and specialized inquiries. In reviewing this book in 1948 Karl Wallace said: "That *Speech Criticism* will direct further inquiry and serious study into the standards and methods of rhetorical criticism is one of its major contributions." This was a perceptive statement and an accurate prediction. The book (as its authors would certainly agree) is not the last word on rhetorical criticism. But it is probably not too much to say that, allowing for its space limitations, it was the latest word as of January, 1948. As may perhaps be inferred from what follows, Thonssen and Baird have referred to and drawn wisely upon material published prior to 1948. And there is reason to believe that many writers of articles published since that date have been influenced in one way or another by the authors of *Speech Criticism*.

One group of articles in the literature here under examination attempts to define rhetorical criticism, to differentiate it from other types of evaluation, and to fix its limits. An early essay in definition is found in one of the first doctoral studies of a speaker-rhetorician, Horace G. Rahskopf's "John Quincy Adams' Theory and Practice of Public Speaking" (1936). Rahskopf describes the task of the critic as an attempt to determine what response the speaker sought, what response he actually aroused, and the relation between the methods used and the response obtained. More readily accessible and still one of the best brief treatments of the subject is Bower Aly's "The Criticism of Oratory" in his *Rhetoric of Alexander Hamilton* (1941). Noting that criticism should be based on the principles of rhetoric, Aly discusses three historic attitudes toward rhetoric—the Sophistic, the Platonic, and the Aristotelian—and adopts the principles of Aristotle as the basis of his own critical system. As a preliminary to this, Professor Aly traces the neglect of oratory as a subject for competent criticism, and the faults of such criticism as there has been, to a failure to distinguish between rhetoric and poetic. He proceeds to draw this necessary distinction, asserting that the creator of poetic discourse is concerned with portraying life while the creator of rhetorical discourse is concerned with influencing it. "The specific requirement of action or acquiescence by an immediate audience," he points out, "determines the nature of oratory and forms the mold of its criticism."

The problem here referred to, the question of the distinction to be drawn between rhetoric and poetic, between speeches and "literature," and the resultant implications for rhetorical as opposed to literary criticism forms the central theme of a series of discussions extending over several decades. As early as 1923 Hoyt H. Hudson, in an excellent article delineating "The Field of Rhetoric," differentiated in this way: "The writer of pure literature has his eye on his subject . . . his task is expression; his form and style are organic with his subject. The writer of rhetorical discourse has his eye upon the audience and occasion: his task is persuasion; his form and style are organic with the occasion." Two years later, Herbert Wichelns recalled these words of Hudson in his classic essay, "The Literary Criticism of Oratory," certainly the most widely read and most frequently quoted piece in our literature of criticism. Wichelns attempted to show what the criticism of speeches should be by showing what it should not be, demonstrating by extensive illustration the results of applying literary standards to rhetorical productions.

Another article on this subject which deserves careful reading, but which is virtually unknown to speech critics, is Brander Matthews' "The Relation of the Drama to Literature" (1898). Writing twenty-seven years earlier than Wichelns, Matthews' purpose is essentially the same. He is pleading the case for both oratory and drama (he considers these two "oral arts" similar in essence), asking that they be judged not as literature only, but in accordance with principles of their own. He notes a tendency to judge all arts by literary principles. The man of letters is generous with his opinions on pictures, statues, plays, and orations—but since he is unaware of the individuality of the different arts, his standards are purely literary. The painter and the sculptor, Matthews observes, have after a long battle won the right to have their work evaluated according to the principles of their art; the orator and the dramatist request the same courtesy. Brander Matthews was influential in securing this right for the dramatic critic; Wichelns and others have gradually won it for the critic of speechmaking.

But the result of these efforts to differentiate literary from rhetorical criticism and to establish the latter as a separate discipline has sometimes been to draw arbitrary and over-nice distinctions which simply will not stand up. We have been prone to make generalizations which serve admirably to distinguish, let us say, the criticism of George Saintsbury from the criticism of Chauncey Goodrich, but which are far from true of literary and rhetorical criticism as a whole. Before proclaiming the independence of rhetoric from poetic one would do well to review such an article as Hoyt Hudson's "Rhetoric and Poetry" (1924), which reminds us that although we can and should distinguish between the two, still there is usually a rhetorical element in poetry and a poetic element in rhetoric. "I have tried to emphasize the distinction between pure poetry and rhetoric," says Hudson, "and then to suggest that rarely do we find them pure. . . ." Other essays, which while recognizing differences, stress interrelationships, are Hunt's "Rhetoric and Literary Criticism" (1935) and Bryant's "Aspects of the Rhetorical Tradition—II" (1950).

In addition to the studies already mentioned, a number of articles seem to be concerned primarily with examining methods and clarifying basic principles. Such articles are of many kinds: a few set forth a general critical methodology; others warn against specific errors to be avoided; several suggest new lines of approach, or provide patterns of analysis for special types of study; some, especially those written most recently, move toward the formulation of a workable philosophy of criticism.

An early warning against "comptometer research" was issued by W. N. Brigance in an article entitled "Whither Research?" (1933). Brigance decried the attempt to scientize studies in rhetoric and oratory through an over-zealous application of statistical methods and recalled Norman Foerster's comment that a similar tendency in the field of literature had "betrayed the cause of letters, caused the scientifically-minded to gravitate to other fields better suited to scientific discipline, and repelled those not scientifically-minded." He called for "a combined historical and critical study of orators and oratorical literature," a method which has subsequently become standard and which was used by all contributors to Brigance's *History and Criticism of American Public Address* (1943). Donald Bryant called attention a few years later to certain problems faced by anyone undertaking such an historical-critical study. In "Some Problems of Scope and Method in Rhetorical Scholarship" (1937), he discussed the questions (1) of criticism and interpretation *vs.* historical fact-finding, and (2) of the individual point of view *vs.* the social. In 1944, surveying twenty years of scholarship in the field, Loren Reid warned of "The Perils of Rhetorical Criticism." Declaring that criticism is not merely a summary of the speaker's ideas nor a narrative of historical events nor a tabulation of devices, Reid reminded the critic of his "primary and inescapable responsibility to interpret, to appraise, to evaluate." The major peril, he affirmed, was "the strong possibility that the critic may produce something that is not criticism at all."

Important among those wishing to bring new methods to the study of speeches are Irving Lee and Martin Maloney. Convinced that "the development of new modes of analysis with varying terminology and apparatus has left some of us in need of reorientation," Lee enumerates "Four Ways of Looking at a Speech" (1942): those of the rhetorician, the semanticist, the logician, and the general semanticist, suggesting that the method of the rhetorician has been unduly stressed by teachers of speech. In "Some New Directions in Rhetorical Criticism" (1953), Maloney proposes as new ways of understanding speech phenomena, four analytic techniques: quantitative and qualitative content analysis, figurative analysis, and intonational analysis. Rhetorical criticism, Maloney believes, is passing through a transitional stage in which "it has not quite ceased to be a tool for making authoritative judgments on the performances of speakers, and has not quite become an implement of research into certain kinds of human behavior." Granting that critics need not "forego the pleasures of evaluation," he clearly favors moving away from

the evaluative and deductive toward the descriptive and in-
ductive.

Several articles have appeared, most of them compara-
tively recently, which outline a methodology or pattern of
criticism for particular types of study. Most of these patterns
have been worked out in the process of preparing doctoral
dissertations and are published in the hope that they may
prove helpful to others engaged in similar critical studies. An
example is S. Judson Crandell's "The Beginnings of a Methodology for Social Control Studies in Public Address"
(1947). Crandell shows how the formula employed by Richard La Piere in his book on *Collective Behavior* can be
adapted and extended into a serviceable pattern for analysis
and criticism of a reform movement. Leland Griffin is also
concerned with the problem of method in rhetorical studies of
historical movements. In "The Rhetoric of Historical Movements" (1952), he poses some questions regarding focus,
scope, standards, and techniques of reporting and provides
some useful answers. Similarly, Earl Cain calls attention to
the problems involved in the analysis of extended Congressional debate and outlines the procedure followed in his own
doctoral study of the neutrality debates of 1935–41 in "A
Method for Rhetorical Analysis of Congressional Debate"
(1954). Other articles describing specific methodologies are
Virginia Holland's "Rhetorical Criticism: a Burkeian
Method" (1953) and Ralph Richardson's "A Suggestion for
a Project in Contemporary Criticism" (1955).

In 1947 Baird and Thonssen wrote an article on
"Methodology in the Criticism of Public Address," the thesis
of which was that the rhetorical critic's appraisal is a compos-
ite judgment, based on the techniques of rhetoric, history, sociology and social psychology, logic, and philosophy. This
article proved to be a brief preview of Part I of the authors'
book on *Speech Criticism,* which appeared the following year.
As has already been indicated, this book (particularly parts
one, four, and five) is the most complete treatment of the

methods of criticism and must be considered the standard work in the field.

The final chapter of *Speech Criticism,* "Toward a Philosophy of Rhetoric," leads at the same time, by implication at least, in the direction of a philosophy of criticism. Several recent essays move, more or less directly, toward the same end. One of the most distinguished attempts to provide a summing up is Marie Hochmuth's introductory essay on "The Criticism of Rhetoric" in the third volume of *A History and Criticism of American Public Address* (1955). In providing answers to basic questions Miss Hochmuth supplements the conventional precepts of classical rhetoricians with insights from literary critics, philosophers, psychologists, historians, and even atomic scientists. The editors of two other recent volumes also provide philosophic discussions of "The Study of Speeches." In introducing their collections of American speeches Baird and Parrish each pose some of the same questions and give essentially similar answers. A significant matter upon which these and other critics do *not* agree, however, provides a point of departure for Thomas Nilsen, author of "Criticism and Social Consequences" (1956). Noting a marked difference of opinion regarding the extent to which the *effects* of a speech should be within the purview of the critic, Nilsen takes his stand on the side of those who include assessment of effect in speech evaluation, but proposes a radically different concept of "effect" from that customarily held. In one of the most original and provocative articles to appear in some time, he develops the thesis that "The evaluation of effect should be a judgment about the contribution the speech makes to, or the influence it exerts in furthering, the purposes of the society upon which it has its impact."

The history of rhetorical criticism which Professor Wichelns found unwritten in 1925 is still unwritten in 1956. Yet some beginnings have been made. The most ambitious undertaking is certainly Part III of *Speech Criticism,* "The Methods of the Critics," though this is far from being a complete history of the criticism of speeches. But the outline sketched by Thonssen and Baird is gradually being filled out. Harding's "The Listener on Eloquence, 1750–1800" (1944) brings together critical comment by diarists and letter-writers on 18th Century parliamentary orators. My monographs, "Some American Critics of Public Address, 1850–1900" (1950) and "Principal Themes of Nineteenth Century Critics of Oratory" (1952), examine the methods and standards of fifty years of American criticism. The essential features of individual critics of speaking are described and evaluated in such articles as Ernest Wrage's "E. L. Godkin and the Nation: Critics of Public Address" (1949) and my "Emerson As a Critic of Oratory" (1953). Analysis of contemporary criticism is found in Karl Wallace's restrained comments "On the Criticism of the MacArthur Speech" (1953) and to some extent in Wayne Thompson's "Contemporary Public Address: A Problem in Criticism" (1954). Admittedly, these are modest beginnings, but it is not improbable that continued interest in this kind of inquiry may one day make Wichelns' projected history of rhetorical criticism a reality.

A list of articles gleaned from neighboring fields which might edify the speech critic can be as long as one wishes to make it. One seeks inspiration where he finds it, and it is perhaps best to leave each to conduct his own search. There is room here only to suggest the fields of literary criticism and rhetoric as being especially fruitful of ideas. Particularly relevant are the works of Kenneth Burke and I. A. Richards, though some find their style more provoking than provocative. Helpful also are Greene's *The Arts and the Art of Criticism* (1940), and such anthologies as Brown's *The Achievement of American Criticism* (1954), and Schorer's *Criticism; The Foundations of Modern Literary Judgment* (1948).

The basic treatises on rhetoric, ancient and modern, need not be enumerated for readers of this volume but a few classic statements should be recalled lest they be overlooked by anyone. Chief among these are Hudson's "The Field of Rhetoric" (1923) and Bryant's two articles entitled "Aspects of the Rhetorical Tradition" (1950), both of which have been mentioned previously. Not yet mentioned, and certainly one of the most important discussions of the subject to appear in our national journal for the past twenty years, is Bryant's "Rhetoric: Its Functions and Its Scope" (1953). Other suggestive writings on rhetoric are those by Natanson, Duhammel, and Weaver, listed below under "collateral materials."

One eventually must resist adding another reference and conclude a bibliography which has necessarily been selective. Perhaps enough evidence has been adduced, however, to establish the point that after a very slow start, scholars in our field are becoming increasingly interested not merely in turning out more and more critical studies of orators, but in examining the act of criticism itself with a view to establishing principles, testing standards, and refining methods.

Not long ago, Everett Lee Hunt, in a review of the Hochmuth studies in public address, commented favorably upon the variety of critical methods employed and expressed the hope that no attempts will be made to standardize the methods of rhetorical criticism. "There is a danger," he said, "that we might draw up a list of the qualities of the effective speaker, and simply plot a curve for each orator, and let it go at that." Many of us, after wading through a spate of undistinguished, unimaginative "critical studies," have felt the imminence of that same danger. But surely the best insurance against the dangers of ossification and standardization is continued inquiry into the nature and values of criticism, supplemented and enriched by new insights from related areas.

Addendum, 1967

A decade has passed since the foregoing bibliographical essay was prepared for the *Western Speech* symposium. No longer does *Speech Criticism* stand as the only full-length volume devoted to instruction in the systematic criticism of speeches, and many new articles have been added to the literature of rhetorical criticism. Indeed, so much has happened during the intervening years that a radical modification of a generalization made in the original essay is in order. In 1957 I called attention to the abundance of articles devoted to the criticism of individual speakers and speeches and the relative paucity of articles devoted to the nature, scope, and methodology of criticism itself. Today it is probably not inaccurate to observe that we have more distinguished essays *on* criticism than essays *in* criticism. Not that the flow of critical essays dealing with speakers and speeches has diminished; it has not. But our allegedly "critical" essays do not seem to be improving in quality or depth of insight, while our discussions of what criticism properly should—or should *not*—be have often revealed remarkable penetration. In short, we seem to have arrived at a situation in which we know more about criticism than we are able to demonstrate in practice. Our essays about criticism are better than our critical essays.

It is the purpose of this addendum to review some of the writings about rhetorical criticism which have appeared since the *Western Speech* symposium was published ten years ago.

These recent writings seem to fall into three main categories. In the first group are pieces describing the critical methods and topics of individual commentators or groups of commentators on oratory. A second group of articles deals with critical method, often proposing a new focus or emphasis for the critic. A third group are highly censorious; the writers of these articles find much to condemn and little to praise in what passes for criticism in graduate theses and speech journals. Usually, though not always, they follow their attacks upon current practice with formulas for modification and improvement.

I

Articles of the first kind are primarily reportorial in nature, and can possibly be regarded as fragmentary contributions to the history of rhetorical criticism envisioned by Professor Wichelns that has yet to be written. These pieces, particularly the ones based upon graduate theses, are usually too brief or too attenuated to be of much help, but they illustrate a kind of investigation that can be interesting and instructive. Dwain Moore's "John Morley: Critic of Public Address" (1958) reports on one of several doctoral studies undertaken in recent years at Illinois to examine the critical methods of biographers, historians, and men of letters. Moore seeks answers to two questions: (1) what aspects of public address most interest John Morley? and (2) what are his methods as a critic? Jerald Banninga discusses the criticism of J. Q. Adams, who has frequently been presented as rhetorician, orator, and teacher, in an essay, "John Quincy Adams as a Contemporary Critic" (1965), based on a doctoral dissertation and drawing heavily on Adams' manuscript diary.

Considerable interest is manifested in journalistic comment on speaking. Hermann Stelzner examines signed articles in five metropolitan newspapers dealing with the speaking of

the 1960 Presidential campaign and generalizes his findings
in "Speech Criticism by Journalists" (1962). Neal Claussen's
"Two Journalistic Critics of Public Address, 1948–1958"
(1963) are the *Nation* and the *New Republic*. Winona
Fletcher's piece on Edwin L. Godkin's criticism of Wendell
Phillips (1964) is useful as a source of severe contemporary
strictures on Phillips' verbal excesses, rather than an analysis
of Edwin L. Godkin's critical methods. Donald E. Williams'
perusal of sixteen campus newspapers in Great Britain
(1965) reveals a body of critical comment on speakers which
is quite unparalleled on the American college campus. These
British critics, presumably students, make direct, detailed
statements about what they consider acceptable and unacceptable in the manner and matter of classroom lectures, student debates, and political addresses by eminent guests.

By all odds the best of these articles on journalistic criticism is Donald Bryant's "Rhetorical Criticism in *The Middlesex Journal, 1774*" (1964). In a London journal, under the
caption "Parliamentary Leaders," Bryant discovered a series
of essays by an unidentified writer. He describes this writer's
"political complexion" as well as his critical topics and
method, and finds his judgments valuable supplements to
those of Horace Walpole and his contemporaries. Bryant
concludes:

> It seems significant of the political values and the operative
> influences in the public life of the time that, broadly conceived
> and described, the qualities and functions of a man as speaker
> should occupy as prominent a place as our critic gives them in
> the total portrait of the public man. That is an aspect of the
> times which, mistakenly, I think, certain recent historians seem
> to find irrelevant.

One further example of the historical report upon critical
methods of individuals or groups is my essay, "The Dramatic
Criticism of Oratory" (1959), designed as a supplement to
Wichelns' earlier essay on "The Literary Criticism of Oratory." Wichelns had analyzed selected nineteenth-century

criticism of oratory "to see what some critics have said of some orators," and discovered it to be primarily "literary" in its approach. This article examines other critical literature of the same period (principally essays, periodical articles, and histories of oratory) and finds the emphasis unmistakably upon the dramatic aspects of delivery. The conclusion reached is that many nineteenth-century critics of oratory erred not in their failure to distinguish between oratory and literature, but in a failure to distinguish between the orator and the actor.

Articles like these which record the kinds of judgments made of orators by critics of the past and present—however unsubstantial and inadequate some of these reports may be— are the stuff of which a connected history of rhetorical criticism may one day be fashioned.

II

A second group of writers look forward, rather than back, and propose new methods, or at least new emphases, for future critics. Here again, these articles, restricted in length by the limitations of regional journals, are often merely suggestive statements of a point of view which look forward to development and illustration in practical criticism. They also tend to be repetitious, several writers sometimes covering much the same ground while employing a slightly different terminology or focus.

Edward Steele (1962) urges the critic to identify the social values held by a speaker's audience—the notions or premises held in the mind, upon which enthymemes can be based. Once this value system is established, says Steele, the critic is in possession of a useful rhetorical tool with which to evaluate the speaker's methods of adapting his propositions to the specific audience. James Backes (1962) presents a similar thesis. He asserts that each society in history has had its *Weltenschauung* or "world view"—be it idealism, materialism, rationalism, or whatever. The critic, in order to place a

speaker in his proper perspective in time, must become familiar with the *Weltenschauung* prevalent during the speaker's
career. Richard Gregg's "phenomenologically oriented approach" to criticism (1966) deals with some of these same
ideas in psychological terminology and contexts. Beginning
with the postulate that "all behavior is determined by and pertinent to the perceptual field of the behaving organism, or in
other words, behavior is not so much a function of the external
event as it is a product of the individual's perception of that
event," Gregg advises the critic to analyze the components of
the listeners' perceptual or cognitive reality—their "image of
reality." The "cognitive imagery" of Hitler's Nazi audience
included the contemptible Jew, the masterful Aryan race, and
the glory of war, while American audiences cherish the image
of a nation chosen by God to lead the way to a better life.

Huber Ellingsworth, in "Anthropology and Rhetoric: Toward a Culture-Related Methodology of Speech Criticism"
(1963), suggests that critics can profitably make use of the
methods and findings of anthropologists in their "study of
cultures at a distance" to provide background for rhetorical
judgments about an earlier period in history.

Seymour Vinocour, who is interested in "Modern Diplomacy and Speech" (1957), lists thirty-five "basic postulates
concerning international speech" (the speaking of diplomats
and other national spokesmen to world audiences) developed
in a seminar on "Speech as a Medium of International Relations" led by Professor Robert Oliver. Vinocour feels that an
international spokesman addressing a multinational audience
deals with unique problems, and that traditional rhetorical
canons may be inadequate or unsatisfactory for describing,
analyzing, and evaluating the speeches of modern diplomacy.
He believes that his postulates "suggest that a different approach to the area of rhetorical criticism may be feasible."

Malcolm Sillars, in "Rhetoric as Act" (1964), sets down
some "basic assumptions" which he hopes will clarify the job
of the critic. His assumptions are that a rhetorical event is an
act, as much as throwing eggs or pulling a trigger. The rhetor-

ical act is (1) related to force, (2) defined by the rhetoric around it, (3) best viewed as part of a movement, and (4) revealed by its techniques. Jon Ericson, replying in the same issue of the *Quarterly Journal of Speech,* states that there is no need to "elevate rhetoric to the status of an act," as Sillars suggests, since it has been so regarded at least since the time of Quintilian.

Two substantial contributions to the study of critical method are the essays of Robert D. Clark and L. H. Mouat, both of which appeared in 1958. Clark uses a review essay on John Garraty's *The Nature of Biography* to advance a favorite thesis of his own that biography can be an ideal vehicle for rhetorical criticism. He recalls Wichelns' dismissal of the biographical approach to the study of speakers because it was concerned with the orator as a man rather than with the man as orator. He notes the proliferation of so-called critical studies in which illustration of Aristotelian topics (including the speaker's personality and training) is substituted for a close reading of the speeches themselves—and he denies that these are either biography or criticism. He admits the force of Wichelns' observation that biographers often neglect or spurn oratory, but adds that "the failure of given biographers to recognize the importance of rhetoric in the lives of their subjects does not, however, force the conclusion that biography is an ineffective vehicle for rhetorical criticism." On the contrary, it is Clark's contention that there is no better vehicle for complete rhetorical criticism than biography, "quickened as it may be and ought to be with creative imagination." Clark's formula for effective rhetorical criticism is implied in his concluding sentence: "If the biographer is more interested in the speaker than in the word, and the student of mass communications more concerned with the word than the speaker, why should not the rhetorician attempt to synthesize the science and the drama?"

Alone among recent writings, Mouat's "An Approach to Rhetorical Criticism" (1958) rejects pluralism and seeks for a uniform approach. At a time when there is almost complete

agreement that criticism need not follow a single pattern and
that the pluralistic approach is the only defensible position,
Mouat looks for a unifying medium, a set of principles to
bind together ancient and modern concepts. He denies that he
is in the market with a favorite formula: "It is not the purpose of this essay to make a brief for a particular set of principles that will bind rhetorical concepts, but rather to urge
that there be a *single* set of principles." The set he introduces,
for illustrative purposes only, is based in part upon Kenneth
Burke's concept of identification. Mouat concedes that the
man, his work, and his times will remain the common topics
of criticism, but believes that "forthcoming studies may be
more fruitful if critics will consider the advantages of a uniform approach."

The Louisiana State University lectures of Marie Hochmuth Nichols, published under the title *Rhetoric and Criticism* (1963), must be prominently featured in any list of
writings on criticism. All of these lectures are well worth
reading, but those most relevant to our present context are
probably "Rhetoric, Public Address, and History," "Theory
and Practice of Rhetorical Criticism," and those dealing with
the rhetorical and critical theories of Kenneth Burke and I.
A. Richards. Professor Nichols' lectures reveal a breadth of
reading, a keenness of insight, a catholicity of interest and
taste, and a freedom from irritating jargon. Not only is she
one of our wisest commentators on rhetorical and critical theory, but she has demonstrated an ability to write first-rate
criticism herself—as witness her final lecture in this volume
on George Bernard Shaw as rhetorician and speaker and her
analysis of Lincoln's First Inaugural Address in *American
Speeches.*

Although it does not deal in any detail with critical
method, Ernest Wrage's "The Ideal Critic" (1957) should be
mentioned here. In a brief article adapted from a convention
speech, Wrage discusses three qualifications of the ideal
critic, and concludes with characteristically eloquent good

sense: "In the long view, the ideal critic is concerned with ventilating and improving public talk. The ultimate justification for his existence is integrity to standards that transcend rhetoric itself."

III

"Considerable doubt has been expressed about our practices in the criticism of public address," says Malcolm Sillars in his "Rhetoric as Act." He names two published articles, but explains that his reference is primarily to "corridor comments." Nevertheless, the criticism of criticism to which Sillars refers —the disparagement of what is passing and has passed for rhetorical criticism—is by no means limited to convention corridor talk. Published articles and books have labeled our criticism stiff, dull, unimaginative, and trivial. Critics, it is charged, have been "too mechanical and classificational in their practices." They have paid too much attention to technique; they have paid too little attention to technique; they have written history, not criticism; they have been enslaved by neo-Aristotelianism; they have tabulated rhetorical devices. Indeed, it is no exaggeration to say that this occasionally savage dismissal of "traditional" criticism as worthless, coupled with vague references to "modern" or "scientific" criticism, has been a distinguishing feature of the literature of the last ten years or so. Most of the critics of our criticism follow their attacks with suggestions for improvement, but without exception they are far more effective in demolishing the old than in constructing the new.

As early as 1951, in a Speech Association of America convention paper later published as "The Critical Method in Speech" (1953), I urged a careful scrutiny of our critical writing, which seemed to me dull, stereotyped, uncritical, and lacking a proper sense of proportion. It was my opinion then that:

as long as critics of public address fail to recognize in their writings that the most important part of a speech is its communicable content—the ideas and attitudes which it conveys—as long as we neglect content and concentrate primarily on counting words, labeling devices, and listing ethical, logical, and pathetic proofs, just so long shall we continue to write for one another and for no one else.

But these were merely sidelong remarks made in passing; a far more systematic and searching critique was offered a few years later by Albert Croft in "The Functions of Rhetorical Criticism" (1956). An examination of critical theses and articles led Croft to conclude that the "standard" approach has four objectives: to delineate the speaking career of an eminent orator, to summarize the propositions found in his speeches, to establish causal relations between speeches and historical events, and to show how speeches illustrate rhetorical doctrines. Croft feels this approach has fatal weaknesses, and he exposes them with obvious relish. The standard approach, he asserts, treats traditional rhetorical theory as a closed, fixed system, and leaves no room for creative theorizing; it identifies and classifies forms and techniques without evaluating their use as tools to accomplish a speaker's purpose; and it fails to show how propositions and audiences are connected, how a speaker uses techniques to adapt his ideas to audience and situation.

Croft's principal purpose, he says, is not to expose weaknesses, but to suggest new objectives and directions. He repudiates the idea of a single pattern (cf. Mouat), but acknowledges the need for common objectives. He emphasizes three functions of criticism: the *historical,* a report of the ways in which speakers' social values have been related to the social values of audiences; the *evaluative,* an assessment of the appropriateness and uniqueness of the idea adaptation displayed; and the *creative,* a modification of rhetorical theory through this examination of the adaptive process.

This article has been referred to frequently since its publication, and has been reprinted at least once. Its influence is deserved for it presents a perceptive analysis of contemporary critical writing and some provocative hints for future critics. But it also demonstrates that it is easier to point out weaknesses in the present practice of criticism than to prescribe specific means for its improvement. And both, undoubtedly, are easier than actually *producing* better criticism.

The years following the appearance of Croft's article brought repeated sniping at the rhetorical critic and his methods. Considerable enemy fire came from Anthony Hillbruner, who shot three rounds from as many journals in a period of five years. In a short piece on "The Rhetorical Critic's Role in Society" (1958) he accused speech scholars of narrow provincialism. He claimed that they neglect the present in their preoccupation with the past, none has a national reputation outside his own field, and none is ever published in national periodicals of distinction. In "Creativity and Contemporary Criticism" (1960) Hillbruner undertook "a general assessment of the status of contemporary rhetorical criticism" and offered "suggestions for its creative and productive development." His assessment is that criticism is flourishing but lacking in creativity, artistry, illuminating analysis, and crystallizing synthesis. Such creative criticism as exists comes not from rhetoricians, but from journalists, literary men, political scientists—from "practically anyone else who takes a fancy to do it." He calls for more attention to contemporary speaking, and maintains that such criticism would result in improved speaking, even as criticism of contemporary literature has exerted a favorable influence on writing. Three years later, in "Criticism as Persuasion" (1963), Hillbruner renewed his attack on dull, unimaginative, chiefly expository or descriptive criticism, and called for "persuasive" criticism,— by which he apparently meant vivid, imaginative, and evaluative writing: "Although one does not need to be a gifted phrasemaker for this task, it helps." In *Critical Dimensions: The Art of Public Address Criticism* (1966) Hillbruner continues his analysis of contemporary critical writing and presents in considerable detail his own suggestions for a more varied and flexible approach to the intrinsic and extrinsic criticism of public address.

In 1962, Phillip Tompkins joined the attack with an article entitled "Rhetorical Criticism: Wrong Medium?" Tompkins begins with the questionable assumption that rhetorical criticism is essentially the application of rhetorical theory to speech manuscripts. Noting the difficulty of representing speech accurately in writing, he dismisses the study of speech manuscripts as "an effort to study critically oral communication received from an inappropriate medium (the printed page) via an inappropriate sensory channel (vision)." He does not recommend abandonment of textual analysis, but places it at the bottom of a hierarchy of research priorities. At the next level he would place the criticism (as listener, not reader) of contemporary speaking. Top priority is given to the experimental study of rhetoric. The speech scholar's most important job, according to Tompkins, is "the criticism of contemporary speech received from the appropriate medium (sound waves) via the appropriate sensory channel (audition)."

In "The Historical-Critical Type of Research: A Reexamination" (1962), Kenneth Hance took note of a host of criticisms of the historical critical method itself, as well as of specific procedures followed by those employing this method, and proposed ways of meeting such criticisms. Nevertheless, despite Hance's valiant defense, the attacks continued. Sillars's "Rhetoric as Act," previously referred to, echoed earlier charges that traditional criticism was stiff, unimaginative, and trammeled by a "classificational strait jacket," and provoked Jon Ericson to respond with "A Critique of Rhetorical Criticism" (1964). Ericson revealed impatience with current characterizations of criticism as "traditional" or "modern" or "scientific." The important thing, he asserted with some heat, is not the label attached to the critical method, but whether the criticism results in useful, insightful conclusions. This proved no deterrent to further assaults upon traditional methods. George Dell (1966) deplored the widespread preoccupation with reconstructing social and historical setting and the failure to criticize the speaker's invention from the perspective of his philosophy. The ultimate objective of speech criticism, he confidently asserted, should be to criticize the truth of the speaker's philosophic assumptions.

All this, however, was relatively minor skirmishing. In 1965, in *Rhetorical Criticism: A Study in Method,* Edwin Black rolled out the big guns for a devastating blast at traditional or as he called it, "neo-Aristotelian," criticism. Indeed, one reviewer (Ehninger) observed that if Wichelns' 1925 essay gave neo-Aristotelianism its birth, Black's book (dedicated, incidentally, to Wichelns), might deal the school its death blow.

The bulk of this little book is directed toward establishing the proposition that "the prevailing mode of rhetorical criticism is profoundly mistaken." The two final chapters profess to provide "an alternate frame of reference," and to multiply the options available to the critic. Black lists the distinguishing features of neo-Aristotelianism as:

> the classification of rhetorical discourses into forensic, deliberative, and epideictic; the classification of "proofs" or "means of persuasion" into logical, pathetic, and ethical; the assessment of discourse in the categories of invention, arrangement, delivery, and style; and the evaluation of rhetorical discourse in terms of its effects on its immediate audience.

He regards this preoccupation with assessing immediate results with a specific audience on a specific occasion as one of the crucial shortcomings of the method; another is its tendency to assume the rationality of audiences, which renders it deficient in dealing with highly emotional discourse. He does not claim to offer a new system of criticism as an alternative to neo-Aristotelianism, but only an orientation to such a system. He is not interested in gauging the immediate effects of a single speech; he wishes to analyze the "process" of given genres of discourse. To this end Black proposes the concept of "a scale of rhetorical transactions"—transactions involving situations, strategies, and effects. In attempting to illustrate this abstruse concept, he begins with a known audience effect—radical conversion, for example—and seeks to discern characteristic strategies which produce this effect, and to describe kinds of situations in which the effect would be produced.

Black's book has been more extensively reviewed than any book recently published in our field; five reviews appeared in a six-month period in the speech journals. Douglas Ehninger (*Western Speech,* Fall 1965) finds the burden of Black's argument against neo-Aristotelianism "irrefutable and its effect devastating," but is disappointed because the promised alternative options are not developed in sufficient detail. The value of the book, he believes, "lies in the decisiveness with which it clears the ground for the growth of new theories of criticism rather than in the nurture of these theories themselves."

Other reviewers, while sharing Ehninger's disappointment in Black's failure to develop further his own critical method, are not disposed to accept without demur his wholesale attack upon the traditional system. Both Robert Scott and John Jellicorse (*Quarterly Journal of Speech,* October 1965) question whether contemporary criticism really displays the qualities Black attributes to it. Scott, for example, notes Black's criticism of the Aristotelian doctrine of emotional appeals and points out that "neo-Aristotelian" critics are most *un*-Aristotelian in their treatment of *pathos.* "They seem quite often to do precisely what Black says Aristotelianism will not allow them to do, that is, to deal with emotion as emotion, not as emotion brought about by and somehow augmenting argument." And Jellicorse denies the charge that contemporary critics concern themselves exclusively with the immediate results of a speech. "While concern for results is inherent in rhetorical criticism," he maintains, "concern for an *immediate* audience is not inherent in rhetorical criticism, Aristotelian or otherwise."

Lawrence Rosenfield (*Speech Teacher,* January 1966) is
perplexed about who it is that Black is assailing: Is it Aristotle himself, or erring neo-Aristotelians? And, making one of
the most telling points scored against the book, he says:
"Even if we grant Black that some Aristotelian concepts are
incomplete for the purposes of contemporary critics, Black
did not show us how this prevents the 'neo-Aristotelian' from
extending Aristotelian principles to encompass modern discourse." *

All the reviewers—including Waldo Braden (*Southern
Speech Journal,* Spring 1966), who regards Black's system
not as an alternative to neo-Aristotelianism, but as complementary to it—agree upon the importance of *Rhetorical Criticism,* and unanimously pronounce it stimulating, insightful,
and provocative.

IV

Having appended to my earlier essay a brief mention of "collateral materials" in neighboring fields, I should perhaps close
this addendum in the same way. Once again, the potentialities are limitless, and I shall add to my list only a handful of
the items I have found most valuable. Chief among these is
Wayne Shumaker's little book on *Elements of Critical Theory*
(1952). Although this book is addressed to literary critics, the
excellent introductory chapter on definition, the distinction
between two principal kinds of critical statement, and the de-
lineation of "internal and external reference forms" for analysis, all have important implications for the critic of rhetorical
discourse. Clearly written with a minimum of technical jargon, this is one of the most sensible and helpful volumes on
criticism that I have encountered.

Helpful also is *Literary Criticism: A Short History*

* In a subsequent article in *Speech Monographs* (1966), Rosenfield
abstracts a "notion of process" from Aristotle's metaphysical writings
and suggests three implications for today's rhetorical critic.

(1957) by W. K. Wimsatt, Jr., and Cleanth Brooks, who
claim in their introduction to have written "a history of ideas
about verbal art and about its elucidation and criticism."
Their focus, of course, is upon poetry or "literature," but
much of what they say is of interest to those concerned with
other forms of "verbal art." Wimsatt's title essay in *Explication as Criticism* (1963) deals with the nature of the critic's
task: Must he make value judgments, or may he simply analyze and compare? Wimsatt's aim is "to talk about the question whether explication of a poem is itself an act of criticism
and hence of evaluation. Not whether it is necessary to understand a poem in order to criticize it . . . but whether to
understand a poem is the same as to criticize it."

To the two books by Kenneth Burke previously listed I
have added a third, his *Counter-Statement* (1931) and suggest
to readers who are puzzled by Burke's esoteric terminology
that they may find in William Rueckert's *Kenneth Burke and
the Drama of Human Relations* (1963) a key to some of the
mysteries.

I wish finally to call attention to a volume which is less
well-known than it deserves to be. *Papers in Rhetoric and
Poetic* (1965) were originally presented at an invitational
conference at the University of Iowa and subsequently published under the editorship of Donald Bryant, who describes
their central theme as "the relevance of rhetoric, however
conceived, in the interpretation and criticism of literature—
drama, poetry, satire, prose narrative and the novel, oratory."
Of interest to critics of public address are Edwin Black's
"Frame of Reference in Rhetoric and Fiction," Richard
Murphy's "Problems in Speech Texts," and, especially, Bryant's admirable essay on "Uses of Rhetoric in Criticism."

V

Ten years ago, I concluded by noting the need for "continued
inquiry into the nature and values of criticism." While I do

not now wish to repudiate those sentiments, the experience of preparing this supplementary bibliography has induced a certain sympathy with Jon Ericson's proposal that rhetorical scholars "might profitably turn their attention from writing (to one another) about the importance of their studies, and direct their energies, instead, to performing the critical act."

We have probably flailed away enough at "traditional" criticism—whatever that may be. We should undoubtedly continue the efforts begun by Black, Croft, Clark, Nichols, and others toward formulating alternative options. But the ultimate fruition of all these efforts, and the test of the efficacy of such essays as are presented in this volume, must be the production of intelligent, imaginative critical writing which manages somehow, whatever the label attached to the technical apparatus, to elucidate and evaluate more successfully than we have been able to do thus far the processes by which men are adapted to ideas and ideas to men.

ITEMS MENTIONED

Aly, Bower. *The Rhetoric of Alexander Hamilton.* New York: Columbia University Press, 1941, pp. 25–32.

Backes, James G. "Rhetorical Criticism: Yet Another Emphasis," *Western Speech,* XXVI (Summer 1962), 164–167.

Baird, A. C. "The Study of Speeches," in *American Public Addresses, 1740–1952.* New York: McGraw-Hill, 1956.

Baird, A. C., and Lester Thonssen. "Methodology in the Criticism of Public Address," *Quarterly Journal of Speech,* XXXIII (April 1947), 134–138.

Banninga, Jerald L. "John Quincy Adams as a Contemporary Critic," *Central States Speech Journal,* XVI (August 1965), 173–178.

Baskerville, Barnet. "The Critical Method in Speech," *Central States Speech Journal,* IV (July 1953), 1–5.

———. "The Dramatic Criticism of Oratory," *Quarterly Journal of Speech,* XLV (February 1959), 39–45.

———. "Emerson as a Critic of Oratory," *Southern Speech Journal,* XVIII (March 1953), 150–163.

—————. "Principal Themes of Nineteenth-Century Critics of Oratory," *Speech Monographs,* XIX (March 1952), 11–26.

—————. "Some American Critics of Public Address, 1850–1900," *Speech Monographs,* XVII (March 1950), 1–23.

Black, Edwin B. *Rhetorical Criticism: A Study in Method.* New York: Macmillan, 1965.

Brigance, W. N. "Whither Research?" *Quarterly Journal of Speech,* XIX (November 1933), 552–561.

Bryant, Donald C. "Rhetorical Criticism in *The Middlesex Journal,* 1774," *Quarterly Journal of Speech,* L (February 1964), 45–52.

—————. "Some Problems of Scope and Method in Rhetorical Scholarship," *Quarterly Journal of Speech,* XXIII (April 1937), 182–189.

Cain, Earl R. "A Method for Rhetorical Analysis of Congressional Debate," *Western Speech,* XVIII (March 1954), 91–95.

Clark, Robert D. "Biography and Rhetorical Criticism" (A Review Essay), *Quarterly Journal of Speech,* XLIV (April 1958), 182–186.

Claussen, E. Neal. "Two Journalistic Critics of Public Address, 1948–1958," *Western Speech,* XXVII (Spring 1963), 84–91.

Crandell, S. Judson. "The Beginnings of a Methodology for Social Control Studies in Public Address," *Quarterly Journal of Speech,* XXXIII (February 1947), 36–39.

Croft, Albert J. "The Functions of Rhetorical Criticism," *Quarterly Journal of Speech,* XLII (October 1956), 283–291.

Dell, George W. "Philosophic Judgments in Contemporary Rhetorical Criticism," *Western Speech,* XXX (Spring 1966), 81–89.

Ellingsworth, Huber W. "Anthropology and Rhetoric: Toward a Culture-Related Methodology of Speech Criticism," *Southern Speech Journal,* XXVIII (Summer 1963), 307–312.

Ericson, Jon M. "A Critique of Rhetorical Criticism," *Quarterly Journal of Speech,* L (October 1964), "Forum," 313–315.

Fletcher, Winona L. "Knight-Errant or Screaming Eagle? E. L. Godkin's Criticism of Wendell Phillips," *Southern Speech Journal,* XXIX (Spring 1964), 214–223.

Gregg, Richard B. "A Phenomenologically Oriented Approach to Rhetorical Criticism," *Central States Speech Journal,* XVII (May 1966), 83–90.

Griffin, Leland M. "The Rhetoric of Historical Movements," *Quarterly Journal of Speech,* XXXVIII (April 1952), 184–188.

Hance, Kenneth G. "The Historical-Critical Type of Research: A Reexamination," *Central States Speech Journal,* XIII (Spring 1962), 165–170.

Harding, Harold F. "The Listener on Eloquence, 1750–1800," in *Studies in Speech and Drama in Honor of Alexander M.*

Drummond. Ithaca: Cornell University Press, 1944, pp. 341–353.

Hillbruner, Anthony. "Creativity and Contemporary Criticism," *Western Speech*, XXIV (Winter 1960), 5–11.

———. *Critical Dimensions: The Art of Public Address Criticism.* New York: Random House, 1966.

———. "Criticism as Persuasion," *Southern Speech Journal*, XXVIII (Summer 1963), 260–267.

———. "The Rhetorical Critic's Role in Society," *Quarterly Journal of Speech*, XLIV (February 1958), 100–102.

Hochmuth, Marie K. "The Criticism of Rhetoric," in *A History and Criticism of American Public Address*. New York: Longmans, Green, 1955, III, pp. 1–23.

Holland, Virginia. "Rhetorical Criticism: A Burkeian Method," *Quarterly Journal of Speech*, XXXIX (December 1953), 444–450.

Hudson, Hoyt H. "Rhetoric and Poetry," *Quarterly Journal of Speech*, X (April 1924), 143–154.

Hunt, Everett Lee. "Rhetoric and Literary Criticism," *Quarterly Journal of Speech*, XXI (November 1935), 564–568.

———. "Thoughts on a History and Criticism of American Public Address," *Quarterly Journal of Speech*, XLII (April 1956), 187–190.

Lee, Irving J. "Four Ways of Looking at a Speech," *Quarterly Journal of Speech*, XXVIII (April 1942), 148–155.

Maloney, Martin. "Some New Directions in Rhetorical Criticism," *Central States Speech Journal*, IV (March 1953), 1–5.

Matthews, Brander. "The Relation of the Drama to Literature," *Forum*, XXIV (January 1898), 630–640.

Moore, Dwain E. "John Morley: Critic of Public Address," *Quarterly Journal of Speech*, XLIV (April 1958), 161–165.

Mouat, L. H. "An Approach to Rhetorical Criticism," in *The Rhetorical Idiom*, Donald C. Bryant, ed. Ithaca: Cornell University Press, 1958, pp. 161–177.

Nichols, Marie Hochmuth. *Rhetoric and Criticism.* Baton Rouge: Louisiana State University Press, 1963.

Nilsen, Thomas. "Criticism and Social Consequences," *Quarterly Journal of Speech*, XLII (April 1956), 173–178.

Parrish, Wayland M. "The Study of Speeches," in *American Speeches*, Wayland M. Parrish and Marie Hochmuth, eds. New York: Longmans, Green, 1954, pp. 1–20.

Rahskopf, Horace G. "What Is Rhetorical Criticism?" in "John Quincy Adams' Theory and Practice of Public Speaking," *Archives of Speech*, I (September 1936), 10–12.

Reid, Loren D. "The Perils of Rhetorical Criticism," *Quarterly Journal of Speech*, XXX (December 1944), 416–422.

Richardson, Ralph. "A Suggestion for a Project in Contemporary Criticism," *Western Speech*, XIX (January 1955), 5–8.

Rosenfield, Lawrence W. "Rhetorical Criticism and an Aristotelian Notion of Process," *Speech Monographs*, XXXIII (March 1966), 1–16.

Sillars, Malcolm O. "Rhetoric as Act," *Quarterly Journal of Speech*, L (October 1964), 277–284.

Steele, Edward D. "Social Values, the Enthymeme, and Speech Criticism," *Western Speech*, XXVI (Spring 1962), 70–75.

Stelzner, Hermann G. "Speech Criticism by Journalists," *Southern Speech Journal*, XXVIII (Fall 1962), 17–26.

Thompson, Wayne. "Contemporary Public Address: A Problem in Criticism," *Quarterly Journal of Speech*, XL (February 1954), 24–30.

Thonssen, Lester, and A. Craig Baird. *Speech Criticism*. New York: Ronald Press, 1948.

Tompkins, Phillip K. "Rhetorical Criticism: Wrong Medium?" *Central States Speech Journal*, XIII (Winter 1962), 90–95.

Vinocour, Seymour M. "Modern Diplomacy and Speech," *Western Speech*, XXI (1957), 201–206.

Wallace, Karl. "On the Criticism of the MacArthur Speech," *Quarterly Journal of Speech*, XXXIX (February 1953), 69–74.

———. "Review," *Speech Criticism*, by Thonssen and Baird, *Quarterly Journal of Speech*, XXXIV (December 1948), 510–515.

Wichelns, Herbert. "The Literary Criticism of Oratory," in *Studies in Rhetoric and Public Speaking in Honor of James A. Winans*, A. M. Drummond, ed. New York: Century, 1925, pp. 181–216.

Williams, Donald E. "Speech Criticism on the British Campus," *Southern Speech Journal*, XXXI (Winter 1965), 83–94.

Wrage, Ernest J. "E. L. Godkin and the Nation: Critics of Public Address," *Southern Speech Journal*, XV (December 1949), 100–111.

———. "The Ideal Critic," *Central States Speech Journal*, VIII (Spring 1957), 20–23.

COLLATERAL MATERIALS

Brown, Clarence A., ed. *The Achievement of American Criticism*. New York: Ronald Press, 1954.

Bryant, Donald C. "Aspects of the Rhetorical Tradition," *Quarterly Journal of Speech*, XXXVI (April 1950), 169–176; XXXVI (October 1950), 326–332.

Bryant, Donald C., ed. *Papers in Rhetoric and Poetic.* Iowa City: University of Iowa Press, 1965.

Burke, Kenneth. *Counter-Statement.* New York: Harcourt, Brace & Co., 1931.

――――. *Permanence and Change.* New York: New Republic, 1935.

――――. *The Philosophy of Literary Form.* Baton Rouge: Louisiana State University Press, 1941.

Duhammel, P. Albert. "The Concept of Rhetoric as Effective Presentation," *Journal of the History of Ideas,* X (June 1949), 344–356.

Greene, Theodore M. *The Arts and the Art of Criticism.* Princeton: Princeton University Press, 1940.

Hudson, Hoyt H. "The Field of Rhetoric," *Quarterly Journal of Speech,* IX (April 1923), 167–180.

Natanson, Maurice. "The Limits of Rhetoric," *Quarterly Journal of Speech,* XLI (April 1955), 133–139.

Richards, Ivor A. *The Philosophy of Rhetoric.* New York and London: Oxford University Press, 1936.

――――. *Practical Criticism.* London: K. Paul, Trench, Trubner, 1929.

Rueckert, William H. *Kenneth Burke and the Drama of Human Relations.* Minneapolis: University of Minnesota Press, 1963.

Schorer, Mark, and others, eds. *Criticism: The Foundations of Modern Literary Judgment.* New York: Harcourt, Brace, 1948.

Shumaker, Wayne. *Elements of Critical Theory.* Berkeley: University of California Press, 1952.

Weaver, Richard M. *The Ethics of Rhetoric.* Chicago: Henry Regnery, 1953.

Wimsatt, W. K., Jr. *Explication As Criticism.* New York: Columbia University Press, 1963.

Wimsatt, W. K., Jr., and Cleanth Brooks. *Literary Criticism: A Short History.* New York: Alfred A. Knopf, 1957.

RANDOM HOUSE BOOKS OF
RELATED INTEREST

Your Speech and Voice
by Arthur Bronstein and Beatrice Jacoby

Speeches in English
by Bower Aly and Lucile F. Aly

RANDOM HOUSE STUDIES IN SPEECH

Argumentation and Advocacy
by Russel R. Windes and Arthur Hastings   SSP1

Freedom of Speech: Issues and Cases
by Franklyn S. Haiman   SSP2

The Oral Study of Literature
*by Robert Beloof, Chester Clayton Long, Seymour Chatman,
Thomas O. Sloan, and Mark S. Klyn
Edited with an Introduction by Thomas O. Sloan*   SSP3

Critical Dimensions: The Art of Public Address Criticism
by Anthony Hillbruner   SSP4

Ethics and Persuasion: Selected Readings
by Richard L. Johannesen   SSP5

Quantitative Research in Public Address and Communication
by Wayne N. Thompson   SSP6

ABOUT THE AUTHOR

THOMAS R. NILSEN is Associate Professor of Speech at the University of Washington. He received his Ph.D. from Northwestern University and taught there before joining the faculty at the University of Washington. Professor Nilsen is co-author of *Perspectives on Argumentation* (1966) and author of *Ethics of Speech Communication* (1966), as well as a contributor to the *Quarterly Journal of Speech* and *Western Speech*. His area of specialization is rhetorical theory and criticism.

A NOTE ON THE TYPE

The text of this book was set on the Linotype in a face called TIMES ROMAN, designed by Stanley Morison for The Times (London), and first introduced by that newspaper in 1932.

Among typographers and designers of the twentieth century, Stanley Morison has been a strong forming influence, as typographical advisor to the English Monotype Corporation, as a director of two distinguished English publishing houses, and as a writer of sensibility, erudition, and keen practical sense.

This book was composed, printed and bound by H. Wolff Book Manufacturing Company, New York, New York.